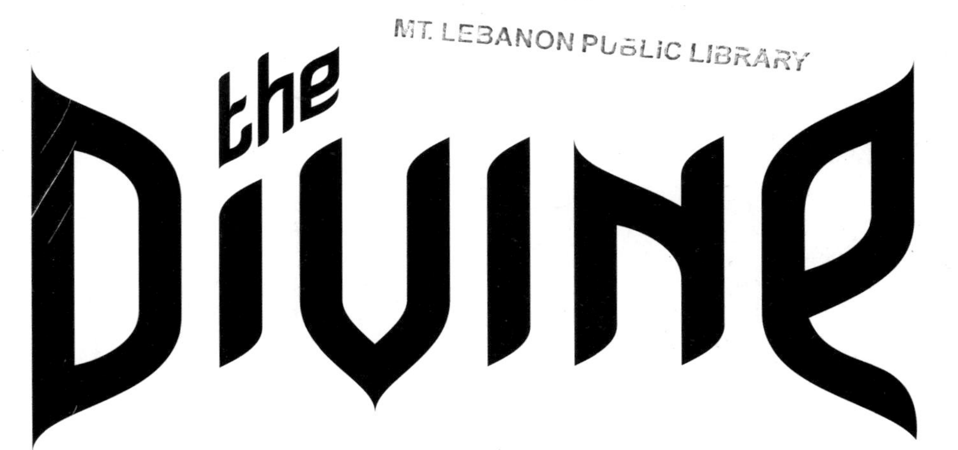

The Divine

Art by
ASAF HANUKA
TOMER HANUKA

Written by
BOAZ LAVIE

First Second
New York

HAVE I EVER TOLD YOU ABOUT THE SMOKE? NEVER SEEN ANYTHING LIKE IT...

COULDN'T BELIEVE IT WAS ME MAKING ALL THAT MESS.

THE ANIMALS RAN DOWN THE MOUNTAIN LIKE THEY THOUGHT IT WAS AN EARTHQUAKE OR SOMETHING.
WE PLAYED A LITTLE GAME WITH THEM.
TAKA
TAKA
TAKA
TAKA

TAKATAKAK
WE SHOT AT ZEBRAS AND BLUE TAIL PARROTS. BAMBIS AND THEIR MOMMIES.

THEN WE SEE THIS THING COMING OUT OF THE SMOKE...

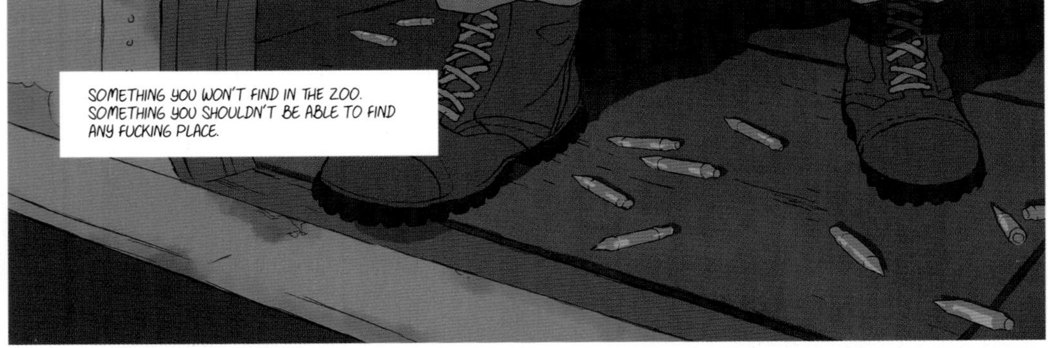
SOMETHING YOU WON'T FIND IN THE ZOO. SOMETHING YOU SHOULDN'T BE ABLE TO FIND ANY FUCKING PLACE.

THEY TOLD ME NOT TO SHOOT IT, IT'S BAD LUCK IN THE FAIRY TALES.

MY 1955 KALASHNIKOV GOES DEAD. SHOCKER.
CLICK
KLANK

SO I SWITCHED TO AN AMERICAN-MADE GUN.

BLAM!!

PUT A BULLET IN ITS EYE.

COULDN'T SEE IF I HIT IT. BUT WHATEVER THIS CREATURE WAS, IT FELL DOWN INTO THE SMOKE.
IT CRACKED THE WINDSHIELD WITH ITS SHRIEK.
CRACK!
SUCH A BRUTAL EXPERIENCE, MAN... TOOK ME HOURS TO GET MY HEART RATE BACK TO NORMAL.
ARE YOU DONE?

WHAT'S THE MATTER? DON'T LIKE MY QUANLOM STORIES?
YOU'RE NOT TALKING ME INTO THIS.

MAN, IT'S EASY MONEY, A CAKEWALK.
TWO WEEKS. 45 GRAND, STRAIGHT FROM THE U.S. GOVERNMENT.

JASON... DROP IT.

YOU'RE A NEWLYWED! I BET YOU AND THE MISSUS COULD USE SOME CASH.
WE'RE DOING JUST FINE WITHOUT ME BLOWING UP MOUNTAINS FOR THE C.I.A.

IT'S NOT C.I.A. AND IT'S NOT BLOWING UP MOUNTAINS. IT'S CALLED LAVA TUBE DENUDING.

WE'RE HELPING THESE POOR PEOPLE GET THEMSELVES SOME FANCY MINERALS.
AND YOU GET TO MEET FLYING LIZARDS!
YEAH, I GOT THAT PART.

DOESN'T MATTER. I ALREADY APPLIED FOR THE OPENING IN OUR DALLAS OFFICE.
GOOD LUCK WITH THAT.
BEEP!

R.D.X. TESTING IN 15 SECONDS.

FIRE IN THE HOLE!

WITH US THIS MORNING: RACHEL ENELOW FROM THE DANCING SUN TRAVEL AGENCY, HERE IN TEMPLE. SO WHAT'S HOT THIS SUMMER, RACHEL?
CANCUN AND JAMAICA ARE POPULAR DESTINATIONS THIS YEAR.
FANTASTIC RESORTS, GORGEOUS BEACHES. BUT DON'T FORGET, YOU'RE ON VACATION! LET THE PROFESSIONALS AT DANCING SUN TRAVEL AGENCY PLAN YOUR TRIP.
LIVE
X
Station

HOW ABOUT ARUBA? A LOT OF PEOPLE ARE TALKING ABOUT ARUBA.
ARUBA IS IS A GREAT OPTION!
THANK YOU SO MUCH, RACHEL. SOME GREAT TIPS FROM THE DANCING SUN TRAVEL AGENCY HERE IN TEMPLE!
AND IT'S BACK TO YOU, JANET!

I CAN'T BELIEVE THEY JUST EDITED OUT EVERYTHING I SAID!
C'MON! YOU WERE AWESOME!
NO, I WAS HORRIBLE, AND FAT.
YOU LOOKED GORGEOUS. AND TV MAKES EVERYONE LOOK FAT—ADDS TEN POUNDS, THEY SAY.
I JUST LOOK LIKE A SWEATY PREGNANT LADY. I SHOULDN'T HAVE DONE THE STUPID INTERVIEW.

I'M HERE. TELL ME ALL ABOUT ARUBA.
CUTE.

THESE LOCAL REPORTERS ONLY CARE ABOUT LOOKING GOOD ON TV.

THEY'RE LIKE MY CUSTOMERS AT THE AGENCY. THEY DON'T CARE IF THEY'RE GOING TO MEXICO OR HAWAII...

AS LONG AS THERE'S DIET COKE.

I'M TIRED. TIRED OF THIS PLACE.
LISTEN, BABE, I GOT SOMETHING TO TELL YOU...
NOT SURE I'M IN THE RIGHT MOOD.

IT'S A GOOD THING.

YOU GOT THE PROMOTION?

MCCALLEN WANTS TO SEE ME TOMORROW.

THAT'S A GOOD SIGN, RIGHT?

YEAH... ALMOST DEFINITELY.

DALLAS!!

SO, WHEN ARE WE GONNA MOVE?

LET'S GET OFFICIAL APPROVAL BEFORE WE START PACKING.

JUST WANTED TO CHEER YOU UP.
IT WORKED!

GIVE ME A SEC, MARK. IT TAKES A MINUTE FOR THESE THINGS TO GO CLEAR WHEN I COME INSIDE.
...STILL DARK?
STILL DARK.

DO ME A FAVOR AND CLOSE THE CURTAINS, WOULD YOU?
SURE.

SO, YOU APPLIED FOR THE DALLAS JOB.

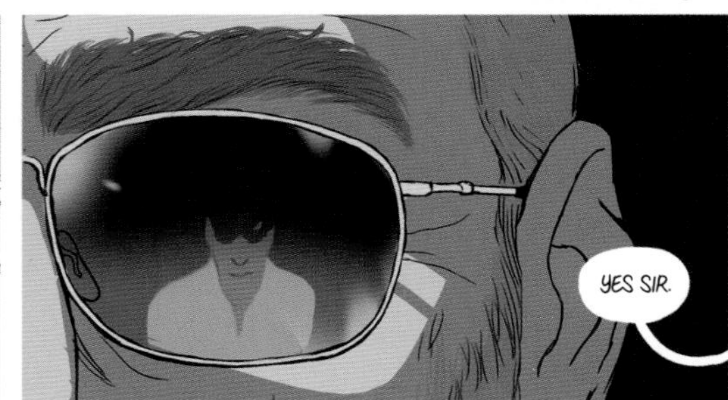
YES SIR.

I'M SORRY, MARK, BUT THE POSITION IS NO LONGER AVAILABLE. DOWNSIZING, THEY SAY.

I SEE.

LISTEN, MARK. YOU'RE ONE HELL OF AN EXPLOSIVES TECHNICIAN.
WE'RE GOING TO PROMOTE YOU. YOU DESERVE THAT.

I APPRECIATE IT.

WE WANT YOU AT OUR EDEN FACILITY.

EDEN?
EDEN, TEXAS. IT'S A MARVELOUS PLACE.

YOU'RE GONNA FALL IN LOVE WITH EDEN. AND YOUR WIFE WILL, TOO.
EVERYONE WHO HAS EVER TRANSFERED TO EDEN HAS LOVED IT! THEY'VE EVEN PASSED UP PROMOTIONS TO OTHER FACILITIES. IT'S UNHEARD OF!

CLEAR.
I BEG YOUR PARDON?

YOUR GLASSES. THEY'RE CLEAR.

YOU SURE THERE'S A BABY IN THERE?

YOU JUST RELAX, OKAY, DEAR?

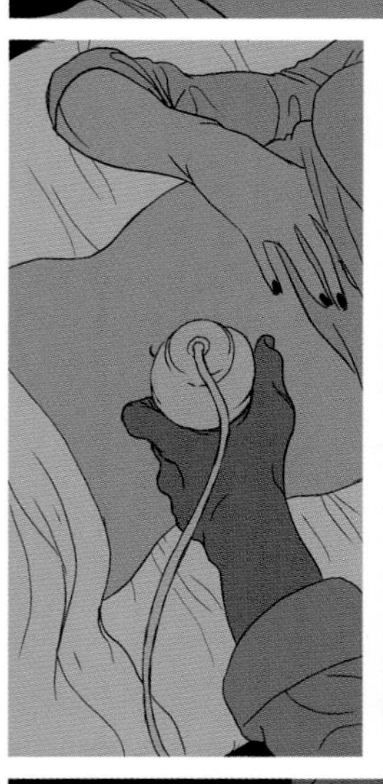

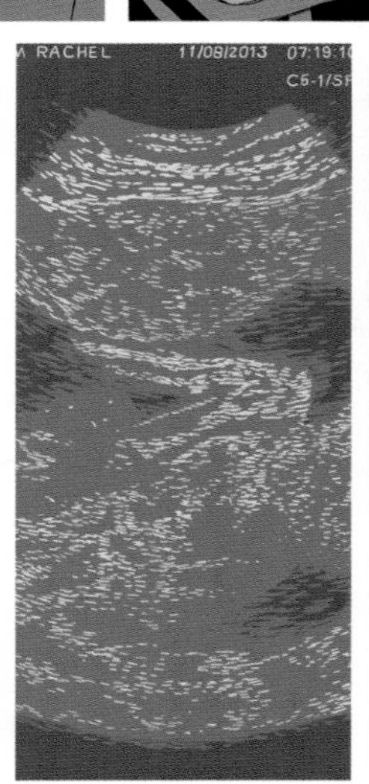
M RACHEL
11/08/2013 07:19:10
C5-1/SF

THERE!
I DON'T SEE A THING.

08/2013 09:19:59AM
C5-1/SFH OB
LOOK CLOSELY...

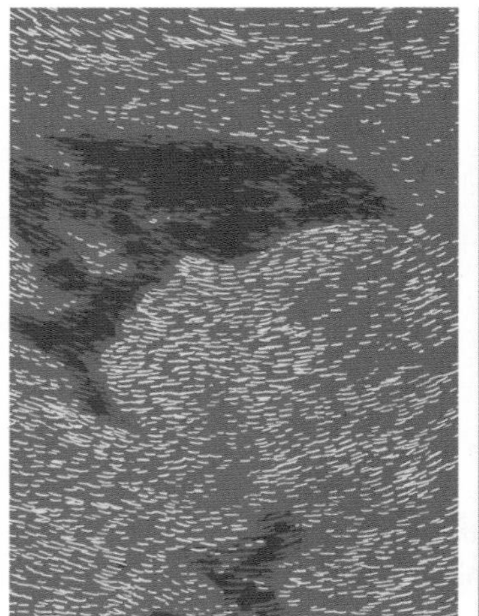

OH MY GOD.

DON'T YOU JUST LOVE DR. RAWI?

YEAH, HE'S... OLD SCHOOL.
YOU THINK HE COULD RECOMMEND A DOCTOR IN DALLAS?

WELL...
PEOPLE PLAN THIS STUFF MONTHS IN ADVANCE.

YEAH, BUT WE'RE STILL HERE, AND WE STILL GOT RAWI.
SURE.

ABOUT DALLAS...

I SAW MCCALLEN TODAY...
THEY REALLY LOVE WHAT I'M DOING. THEY'RE GOING TO PROMOTE ME.

THAT'S WONDERFUL, BABE!

ONLY THING IS, THEY CANCELLED THE DALLAS OPENING. THEY'RE SENDING US TO EDEN.
EDEN, TEXAS. IT'S SUPPOSED TO BE GREAT.

EDEN? I'VE BEEN THERE.

HALF OF IT IS JUST A HUGE DETENTION CENTER. IT'S NOT EVEN A REAL PLACE. IT'S JAILVILLE.

YOU SERIOUSLY THINK THEY'D CALL A NICE PLACE EDEN?

Google

ede

Google Search   I'm Feeling Lucky

Google.com offered in: Spanish

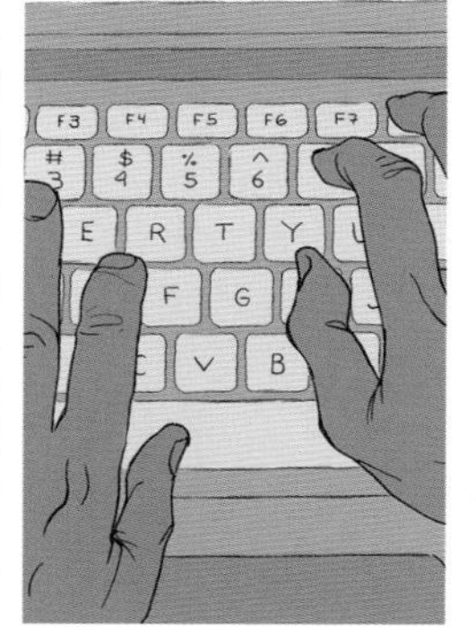

quanlo
quanlot
quan lot nam
quanlong machine
quanlotmong

ogle
quanlom
Web
Images
About 135,000,000 re

LAND OF MY DREAMS.

I WAS JUST CHECKING THE SPELLING. "QUANLOM" IS A FUNNY NAME.

SURE, BUDDY. WELL, IT'S TOO BAD YOU'RE NOT COMING.
BEEP
THE A.G.C. JUST TOLD ME THEY'RE UPPING MY PAYCHECK BY 22 GRAND. "RISK PREMIUM."

APPARENTLY THERE'S A WAR GOING ON OVER THERE.
OH AND A.G.C. STANDS FOR AGENCY FOR GEOLOGICAL COLLABORATION.
SEE? I TRUST YOU SO I TELL YOU.
AND IT'S TOO LATE TO JOIN ANYWAY.

EXPLOSIVES WORK AREA
AREN'T YOU AFRAID YOU'LL GET HURT?

NAH, THAT PLACE IS SAFER THAN CANADA. IT'S FUCKING HEAVEN, I'M TELLING YOU.

WHAT ABOUT THAT WAR?

BULLSHIT.
SOME KID PROBABLY HIT THE MAYOR'S HEAD WITH A COCONUT.

War Zone!
HAHAHA...

WHAT'S THAT?

AN EXPLOSION-PROOF FLASH-LIGHT. BOUGHT IT TODAY.

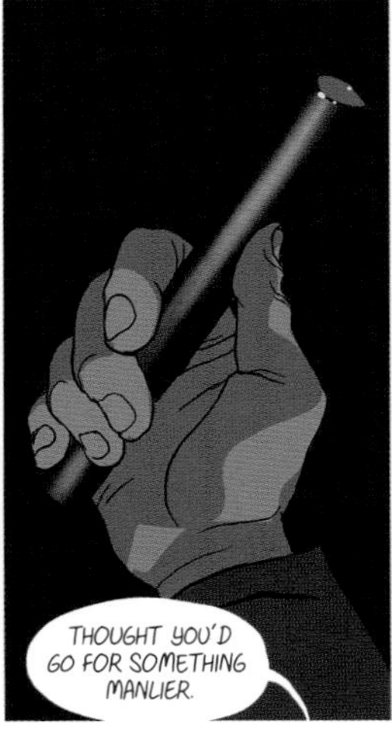
THOUGHT YOU'D GO FOR SOMETHING MANLIER.

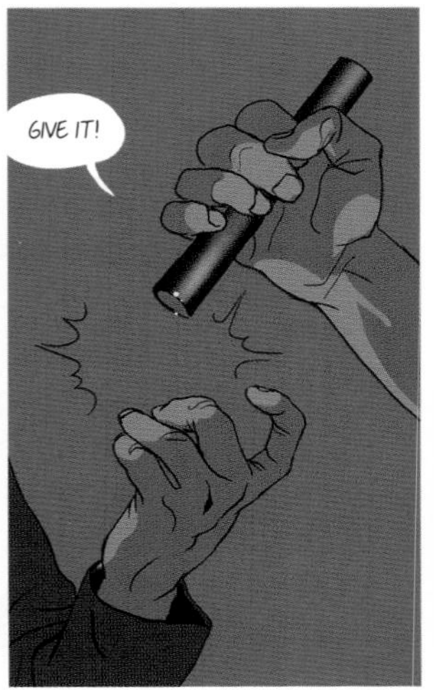
GIVE IT!

CLICK!

IT DOESN'T GET MANLIER THAN THIS, MARK.

AND YOU KNOW WHAT ELSE I GOT FOR MY TRIP?

AN R.P.G. LAUNCHER?

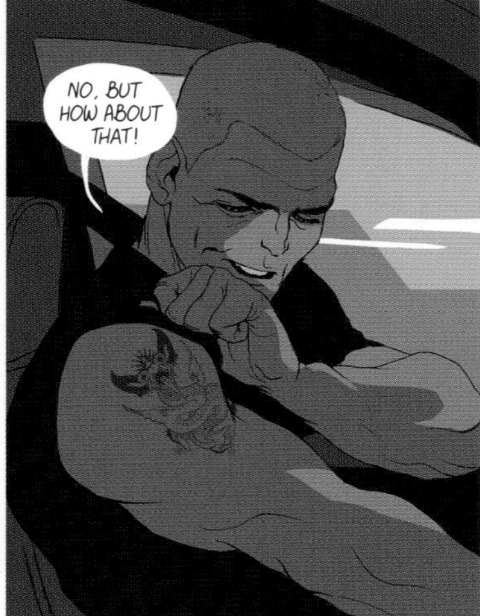
NO, BUT HOW ABOUT THAT!

JUST TOOK OFF THE BANDAGES.

CAN'T REALLY SEE...
SO USE THE DAMN FLASHLIGHT.

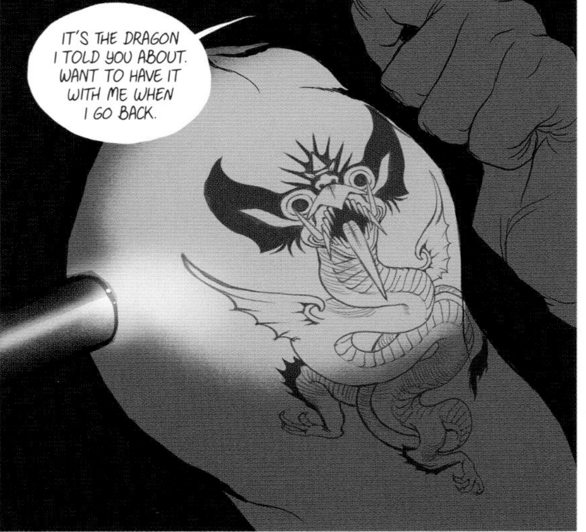
IT'S THE DRAGON I TOLD YOU ABOUT. WANT TO HAVE IT WITH ME WHEN I GO BACK.

YOU GETTING A NOSE RING NEXT? C'MON, IT'S JUST A JOB.

IT SYMBOLIZES MY POWER. I SHOT IT. IT HAS A PART OF ME IN IT.
SURE...

BUT YOU— YOU GOT NO POWER, NO MONEY, NO BALLS.

THAT'S WHY YOU'RE MAKING FUN OF MY DRAGON.

MARK?

MARK... CAN YOU HEAR ME?
WAKE UP!

GOD... PLEASE.

WE GOTTA GO!

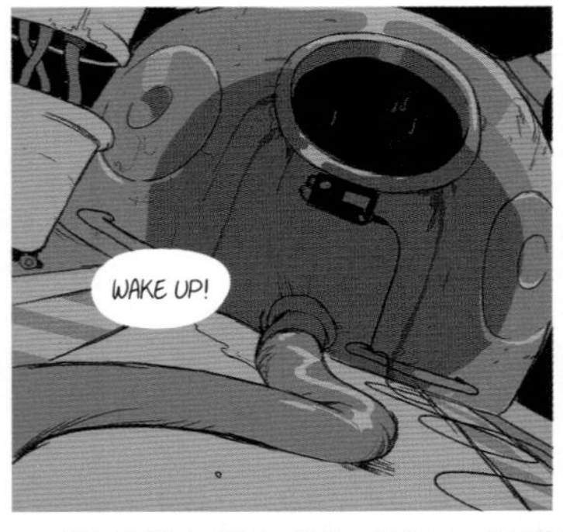
WAKE UP!

MARK, IT'S TIME!

HONEY, YOU HAVE LIKE 8 MONTHS TO GO...

7:55

IT'S HAPPENING NOW! CAN'T YOU SEE?

JESUS.
huff... hufff huff...

YOU READY?

WAIT...
6:59

IT HURTS. I'M HAVING...huff... CONTRACTIONS.

WHERE... ARE WE?
6:51

MARK, PLEASE!

THIS PLACE IS DESERTED. IT'S THE MIDDLE OF THE NIGHT...

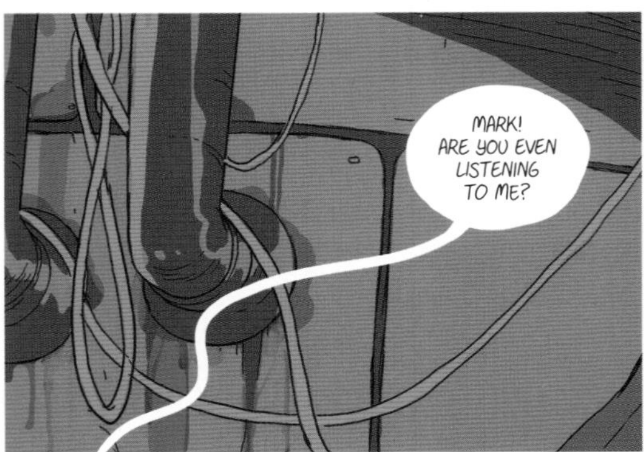
MARK! ARE YOU EVEN LISTENING TO ME?

THE TIMER HAS TO RESET ITSELF BEFORE THE DOOR WILL OPEN.

0:03
MARK!!

0:01

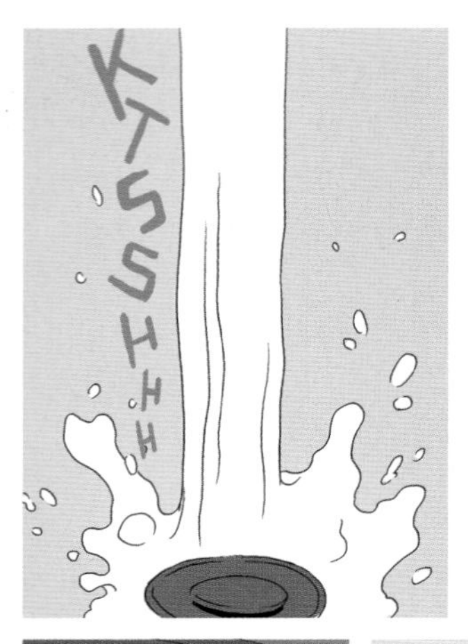
KTSSHHHH

12:34

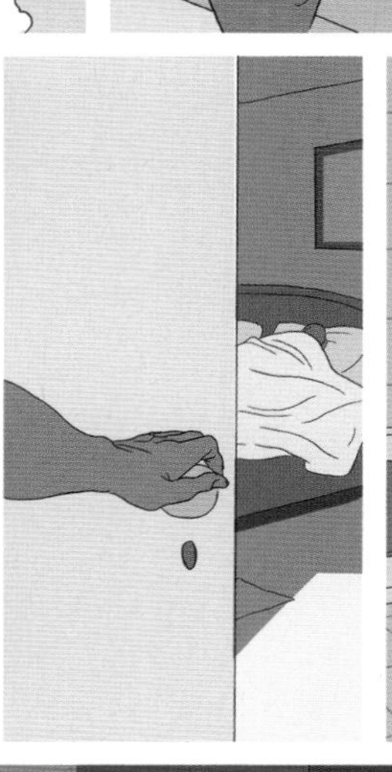

HEY, WHAT'S UP?
Lite
58
CAN'T HEAR YOU, MAN, SPEAK UP!
COMING WHERE?

I KNEW IT! YOU WERE JUST PLAYING HARD TO GET, WEREN'T YOU, YOU LITTLE CUNT!
OKAY, LISTEN: JUST LET THE OFFICE KNOW YOU'RE TAKING THE HOLIDAYS OFF—
ALL YOUR VACATION DAYS, SICK DAYS, ANYTHING YOU GOT.

30% ON THE SPOT, THE REST WHEN WE'RE BACK.

IT'S LEGIT GOVERNMENT MONEY. MILITARY. BUT YOU'LL HAVE TO SHAVE YOUR HEAD.
LIKE THE MARINES, YOU KNOW THE DRILL.

HAHA! I'M JUST FUCKING WITH YOU.
BUT SERIOUSLY, DON'T MENTION THE DESTINATION TO ANYONE.

IT'S KIND OF AN UNDER-THE-RADAR THING. THINK OF IT AS BLACK OPS.
SHITHOLE GOT NO DIPLOMATIC RELATIONS WITH AMERICA, SO BEST TO KEEP YOUR MOUTH SHUT.

GOING WHERE?
VIETNAM.
VIETNAM? WHAT ABOUT EDEN?
THEY ASKED ME LAST MINUTE. IT'S JUST GONNA BE TWO WEEKS. SPECIAL JOB, NICE PAYCHECK. THOUGHT WE COULD PUT IT TOWARD A HOUSE.
SO I SAID YES.
IT'S JUST SO SUDDEN. YOU COULDN'T TALK TO ME FIRST?
IT'S REALLY NO BIG DEAL, HONEY, JUST WORK STUFF. YOU DON'T TALK TO ME EVERY TIME YOU SEND SOMEONE TO BARBADOS.
SO LEAVING YOUR PREGNANT WIFE FOR TWO WEEKS IS NO BIG DEAL?
I'M DOING IT FOR US. WE NEED THE MONEY.

I DON'T CARE ABOUT THE MONEY.

I'LL CALL YOU WHEN I CAN, BUT IT'S HARD TO GET A CALL THROUGH TO THE U.S. OUT THERE.
DON'T BOTHER CALLING.

I GET IT. YOU'RE PISSED.

DAMMIT, MARK, YOU TELL ME WE'RE MOVING TO DALLAS, THEN EDEN, NOW YOU'RE GOING TO VIETNAM?
WHAT DO YOU WANT ME TO DO?

JUST... PROMISE YOU'LL BE HERE WHEN THE BABY COMES.

I PROMISE, HONEY...

YOU'RE BLEEDING.

STUPID AIRPORT SECURITY. THEY HAVE NO IDEA.

THEY SEARCHED YOU?
YEAH, FULL BODY SEARCH. THOUGHT I HAD SOMETHING ON ME. IDIOTS.

DO YOU?

EVEN IF I DID THEY'D NEVER FIND IT.

AND WHAT IS THIS MYSTERY WEAPON?
ANYTHING.

WHAT ARE YOU TALKING ABOUT?
ANYTHING CAN BE A WEAPON IN THE RIGHT HANDS.

HERE, GRAB SOMETHING OUT OF MY BAG.

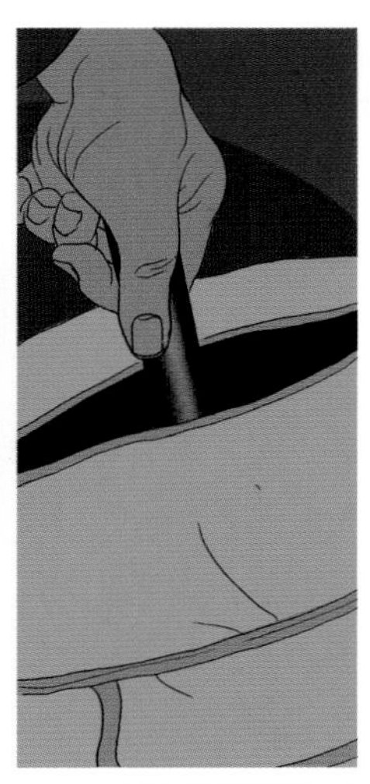

I KNOW THIS ONE. ARE YOU GONNA BLIND PASSENGERS TO DEATH WITH IT?

YOU SEE THIS POINT ON MY NECK HERE?
IT'S CALLED THE SHUITU POINT. IF YOU PRESS IT HARD ENOUGH WITH ANYTHING, EVEN A PEN, YOU'D KILL ME.

GOTCHA.

TRY IT. I MEAN, JUST TOUCH IT.
NO WAY, MAN! GET OFF!

JUST PUT YOUR FING—
FLIGHT 423 TO BANGKOK NOW BOARDING AT GATE C12
THAT'S US.

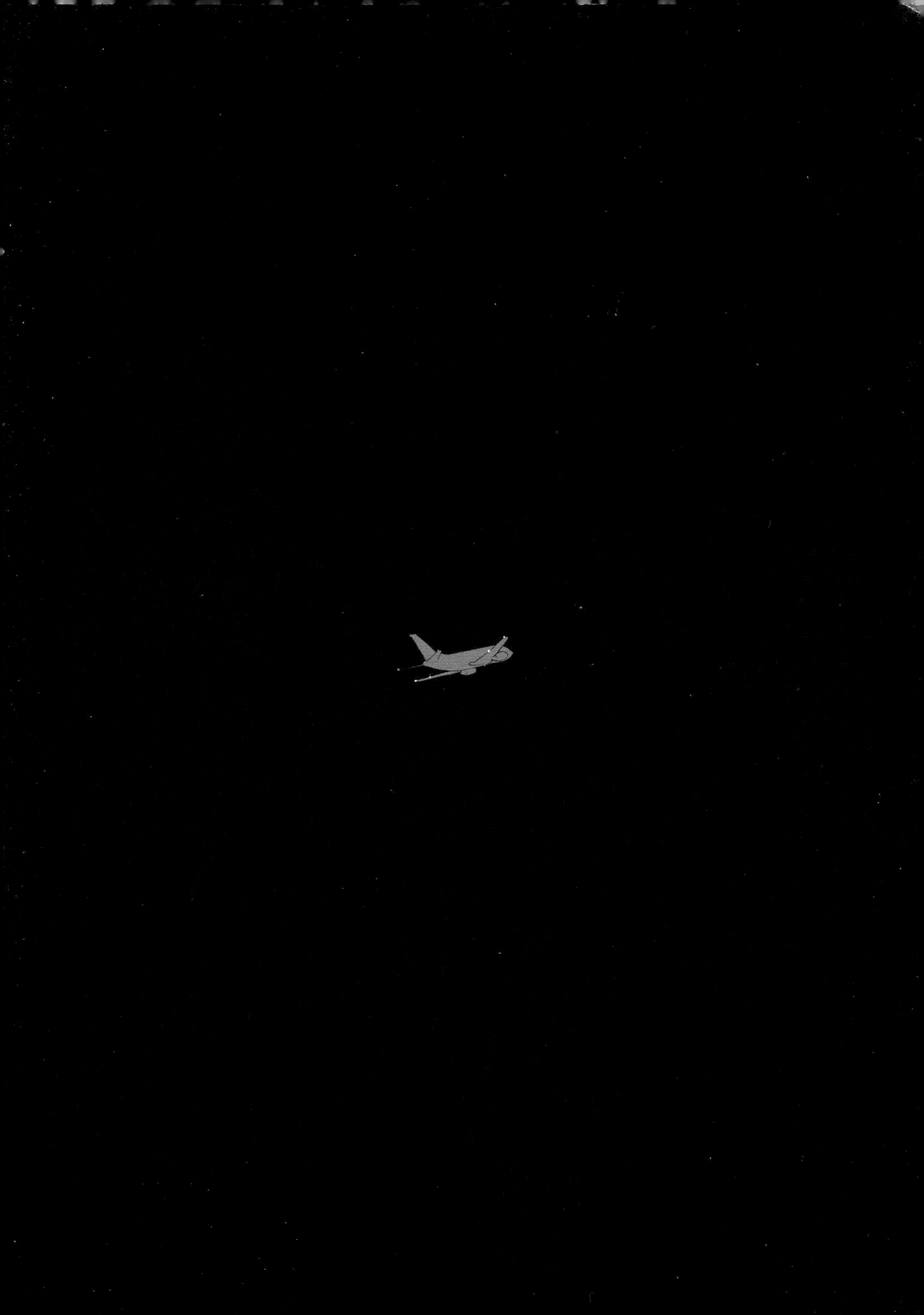

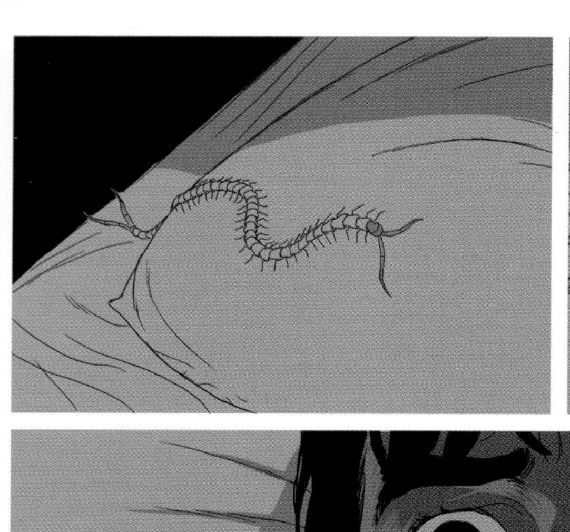

SWATTT

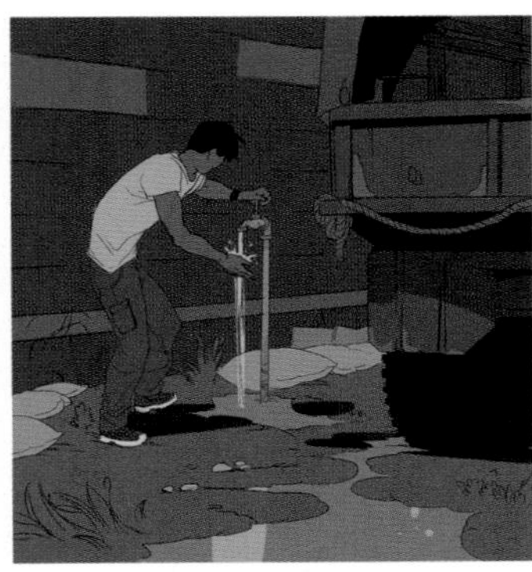

YOU'LL NEED SOME BLEACH TO TAKE THAT OFF.

SINCE WHEN DO YOU SMOKE?
WHENEVER I'M NOT IN THE STATES.

DO YOU ALSO STOP SLEEPING WHEN YOU LEAVE THE COUNTRY?

PRETTY MUCH. THE JUNGLE IS MY RED BULL.
HAVE FUN. SEE YOU IN THE MORNING.

ALL RIGHT, LADIES

PLOTCH!

I'M ONLY GOING TO BRIEF YOU ONCE.

WE WILL DESCEND APPROXIMATELY FIFTY FEET INTO THE LAVA TUBE.

IT'S GONNA BE VERY DARK IN THERE.

SO WE ARE GONNA HAVE TO TRUST EACH OTHER.

TWO MEN WILL MONITOR THE ENTRANCE. FOUR WILL FOLLOW ME INSIDE.

WHEN IT'S ALL DONE WE JUST NEED TO MAKE SURE THE RECEIVER IS FULLY EXPOSED.

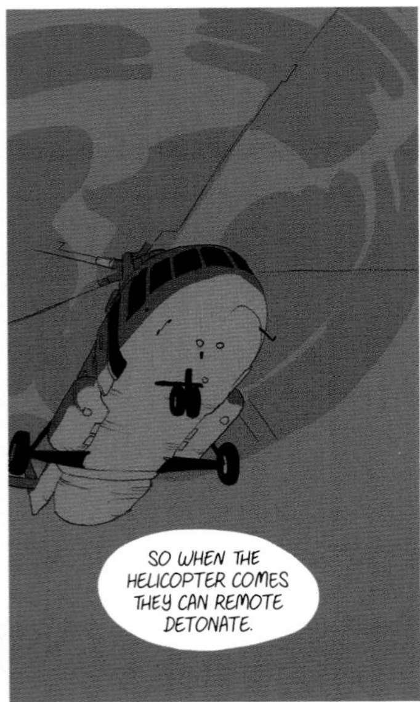
SO WHEN THE HELICOPTER COMES THEY CAN REMOTE DETONATE.

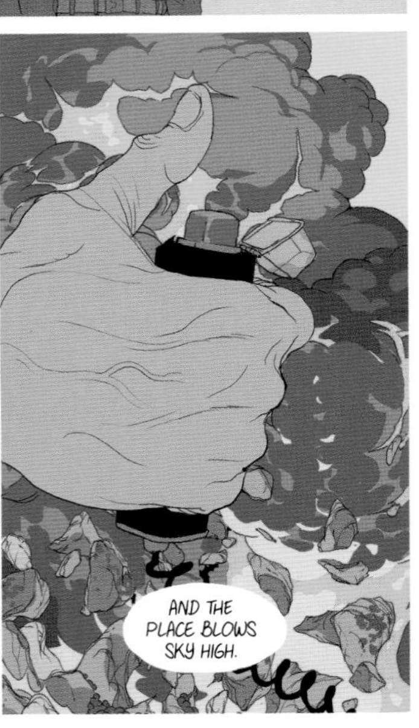
AND THE PLACE BLOWS SKY HIGH.

IF ANYTHING GOES WRONG, AT ANY POINT IN THIS MISSION—
MY BUDDY HERE IS AN EX-CON WITH FOUR MURDER CONVICTIONS. HE'LL MAKE YOU REGRET THE DAY YOU WERE BORN.

WHAT THE HELL, JASON?

BETTER TO BE FEARED THAN LOVED.

TRANSLATOR!
THEY'RE ALL YOURS.
YES, SIR!

SHH!!!

CAN I HAVE PERMISSION TO KILL HIM, SIR?

LET'S STAY FOCUSED ON THE MISSION.
WHAT DO WE CARE?
GO FOR IT. JUST MAKE IT FAST. WE'RE IN A HURRY.
THANK YOU, SIR. IT'S VERY GOOD MEAT.

THOK!

TCH!

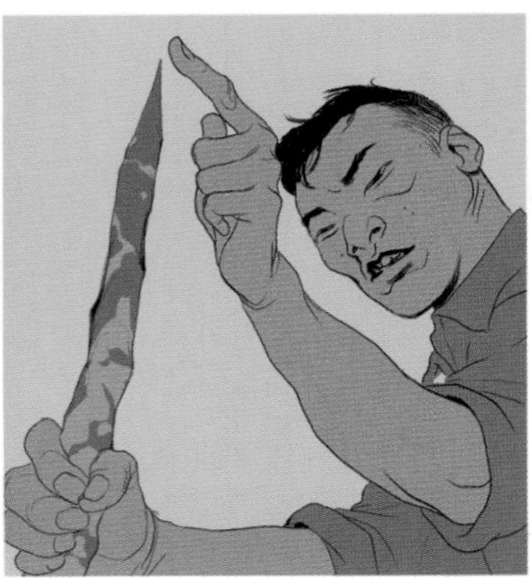

SPORCH!

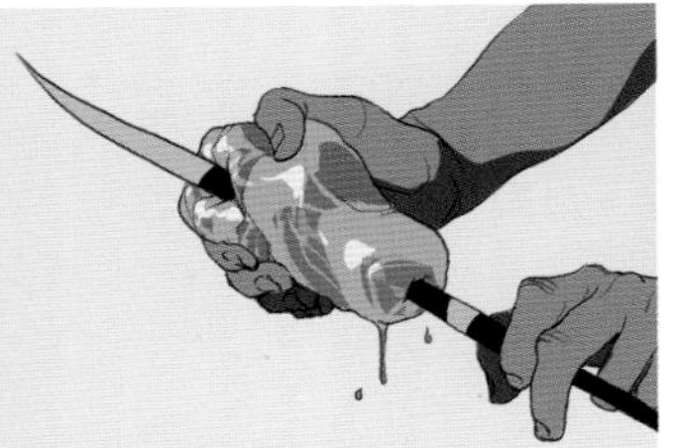

YOU DON'T KNOW WHAT YOU'RE MISSING.

THEY COULD GIVE ME ANOTHER 20 GRAND AND I STILL WOULDN'T TOUCH THAT CRAP.

ALL YOU CARE ABOUT IS MONEY.

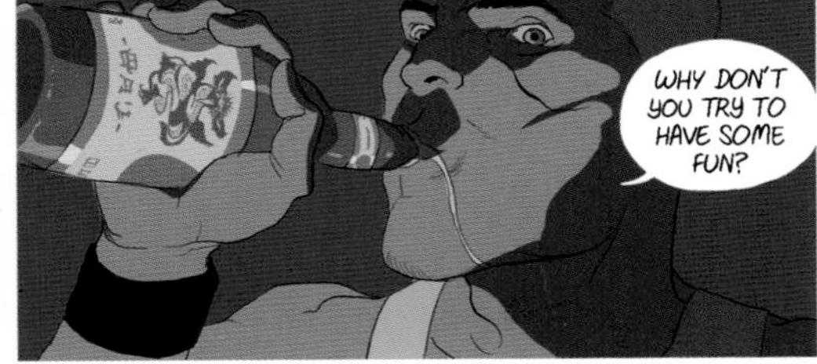
WHY DON'T YOU TRY TO HAVE SOME FUN?

POW!

WHA...

IMAGINE I WAS VIETCONG. YOU'D BE M.I.A. BY NOW.

VIETCONG?
YOU KNOW, THE BAD GUYS. ANY ONE OF THEM.

YOU'RE THE ONLY BAD GUY HERE.
WE'RE GOING DOWN THE TUBE IN TEN MINUTES. EVERYONE IS READY BUT YOU.

OKAY, TWO OF YOU STAY HERE AND KEEP IN CONTACT WITH THE CAMP GUARDS.
FOUR ARE COMING WITH US. I'LL LET YOU DECIDE WHO.
TRANSLATE.

YOU STAY HERE.

THIS UGLY CHIMP HERE.
YOU STUPID COCONUT FUCKER HERE.

AND YOU FAT PIECE OF...
JASON!

WHY THE HELL ARE YOU TALKING TO THEM LIKE THAT?

LAY OFF. IT'S NOT LIKE THEY CAN UNDERSTAND ME.

JASON, THEY ALL SPEAK ENGLISH, THEY'RE JUST ASHAMED OF HOW IT SOUNDS, SO THEY USE THEIR FRIEND AS A FAKE TRANSLATOR.

NO WAY, THEY DON'T HAVE A FUCKING CLUE.

AM I WRONG? ANSWER IF YOU UNDERSTAND ME!

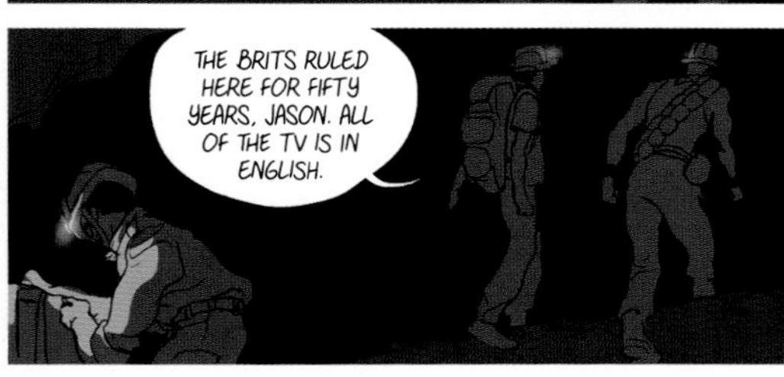
THE BRITS RULED HERE FOR FIFTY YEARS, JASON. ALL OF THE TV IS IN ENGLISH.

OKAY, THEN. I APOLOGIZE, YOU GUYS!

HOW COME BOTH OUR HELMET LIGHTS ARE DEAD?

SOVIET EQUIPMENT. SOMETHING WITH THE AIR. WE'LL HAVE TO COMPLETE THE MISSION IN THE DARK.

RIGGING EXPLOSIVES IN THE DARK? ARE YOU CRAZY?

YOU SCARED?
-SIGH-

YOU'RE GONNA BE A FATHER, MARK. YOU CAN'T LET YOUR BALLS SHRIVEL UP BECAUSE IT'S DARK.
SEE YOU LATER.

GOOD THING I BROUGHT THIS EXPLOSION-PROOF FLASHLIGHT!
MADE IN PITTSBURGH!
CLICK!

THIS BRIGHT ENOUGH FOR YA?
IT'S FINE.
NOW LET'S GET THIS OVER WITH.

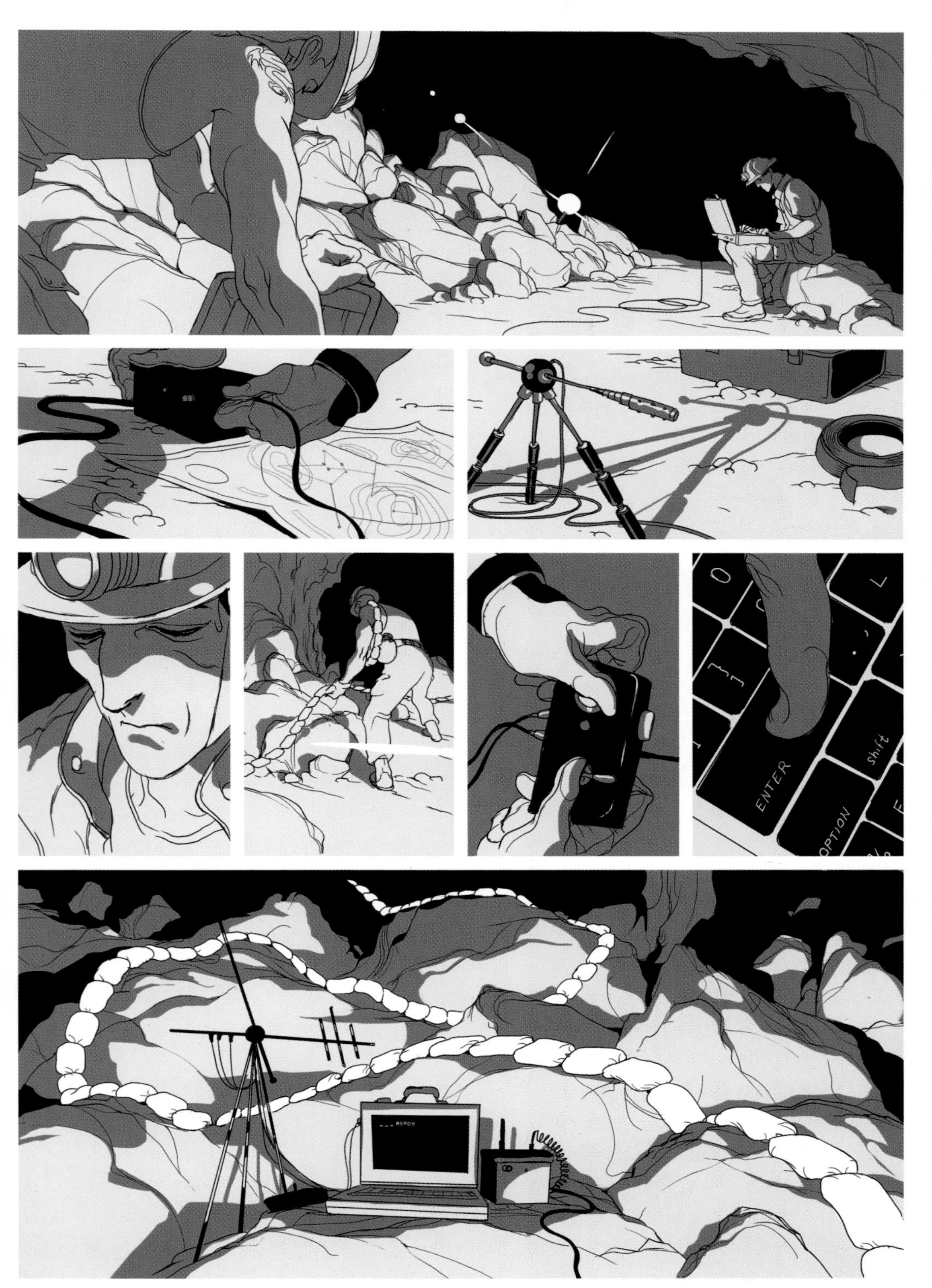
ENTER
shift
OPTION
READY

PLEASE CONNECT ME TO COLONEL TUAH.
HELLO, COLONEL. MISSION ACCOMPLISHED. YOU CAN GET YOUR CHOPPER OVER HERE AND DETONATE THE EXPLOSIVES.

EXCUSE ME?

WHAT'S UP?

A WEEK??
FUCK...

HE SAYS THEIR ONLY CHOPPER IS DEAD, THEY NEED TO GET A NEW ONE FROM CHINA...
OKAY, SO THEY FUCKED UP.

SIR, YOU DON'T NEED US HERE FOR THE DETONATION. THE TUBE IS 100% RIGGED, YOU CAN BRING YOUR CHOPPERS NEXT YEAR FOR ALL I CARE. ANTENNA IS READY, JUST PUSH THE FRIGGIN' BUTTON.

THANK YOU, SIR. GOOD LUCK.

WE'RE GOOD. LEAVING QUANLOM IN THREE DAYS AS PLANNED.

ffft
YOU THINK THEY CAN REMOTE DETONATE WITHOUT US HERE?

FUCK IF I CARE. WE DID OUR PART. IF THE CHOPPER GETS THERE ON TIME WE'LL JOIN IN. IF IT DOESN'T...

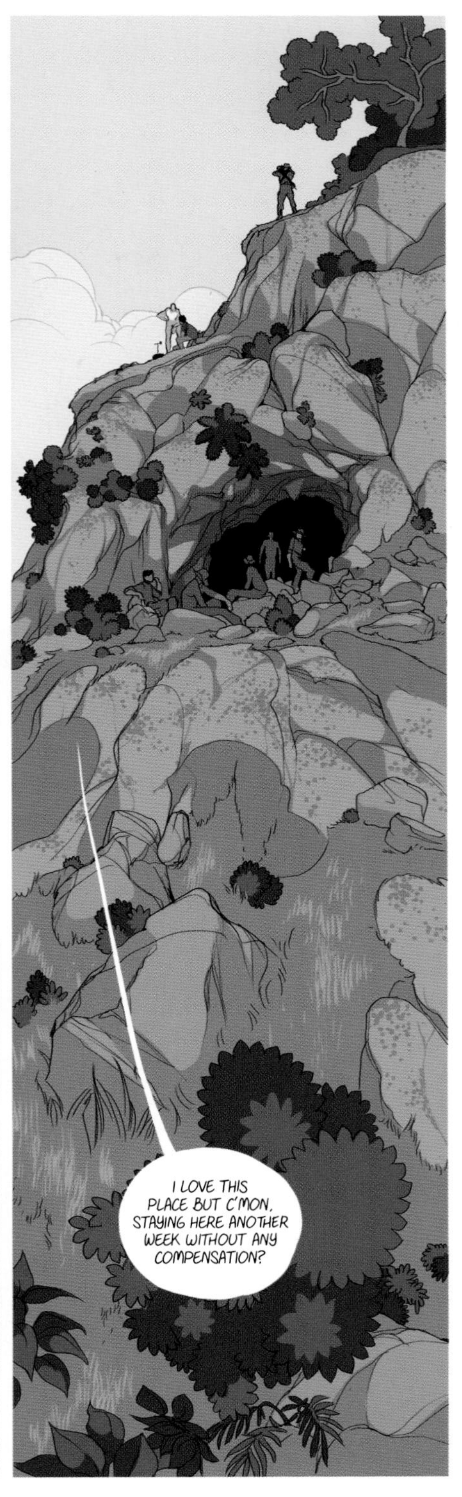
I LOVE THIS PLACE BUT C'MON, STAYING HERE ANOTHER WEEK WITHOUT ANY COMPENSATION?

SIR, LOOK PLEASE.
WHAT IS IT?

PROBABLY NOTHING, SIR.

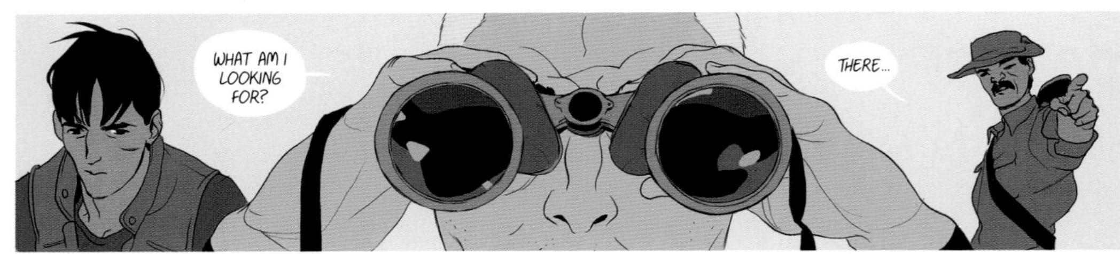
WHAT AM I LOOKING FOR?
THERE...

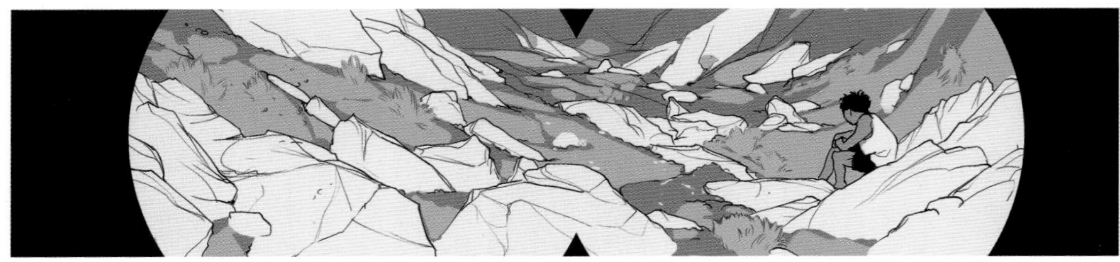

WELL...

WHAT IS IT?
A BOY.

NOT OUR PROBLEM.
GIVE ME THAT!

THE BOY COULD BE HURT.
OH, C'MON.
COULD BE HURT, COULD BE DEAD, COULD BE SLEEPING, COULD BE HIGH ON CRACK, ANYTHING.

AND YOU WANNA CLEAR TEN MILES OF JUNGLE TO CHECK ON THIS LITTLE PUNK? FUCKING HELL...
FINE, MARK.

GIVE ME WATER.

IT'S OKAY. WE WON'T HURT YOU.

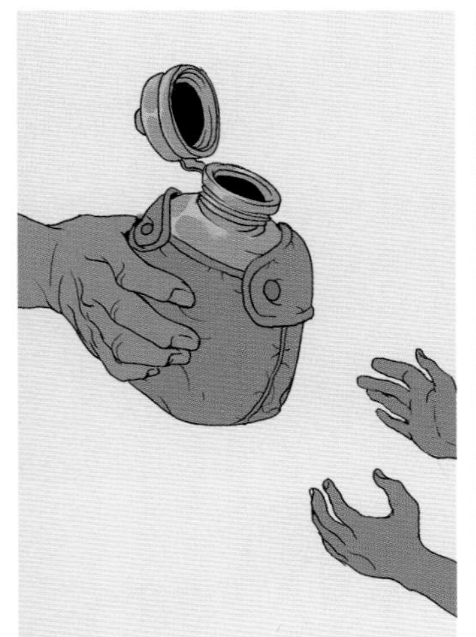

KID LOOKS FINE. WE BETTER MOVE ON.

WE'RE TAKING HIM WITH US.
YOU KIDDING ME?

LET'S HAVE THE MEDIC TAKE A LOOK AT HIM.
THAT IS NOT OUR MISSION.

I DON'T CARE IF HE HAS AIDS AND TWO BROKEN LEGS! HE IS NOT COMING WITH US.

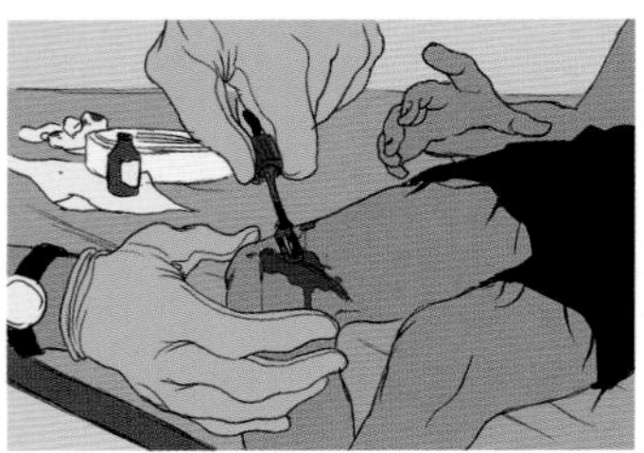

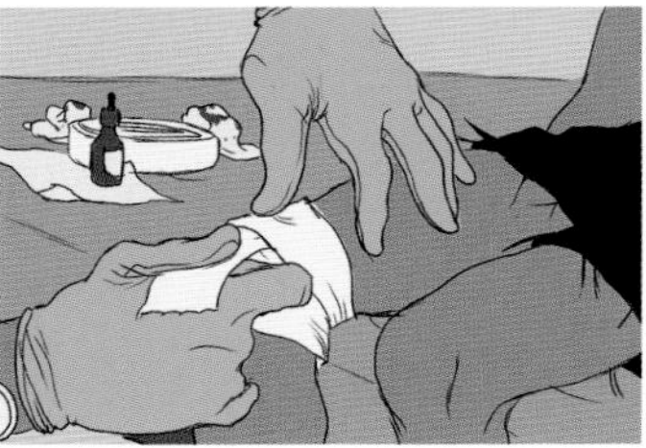

WHAT ARE YOU TELLING HIM?

THAT HE SHOULD BE MORE CAREFUL AROUND THE MINES.

I DIDN'T KNOW THERE WERE LAND MINES AROUND HERE.

JUST A FEW.
DID YOU KNOW THERE WERE MINES, JASON?

THE LIVE MINES ARE SCATTERED IN THIS AREA.

THIS IS UNREAL. WHY DIDN'T THEY TELL US?

CALM DOWN, MAN, WE HAVE THEIR PEOPLE GUIDING US. THEY'RE NOT GOING TO GET US BLOWN UP.

ARE THERE LIVE MINES HERE?
I...I DON'T KNOW.

HEY, PAL. WHERE DO YOU LIVE?
SOA-KOI.

OKAY, WE'LL TAKE YOU HOME.

I NEED TO HAVE A WORD WITH YOU OUTSIDE.

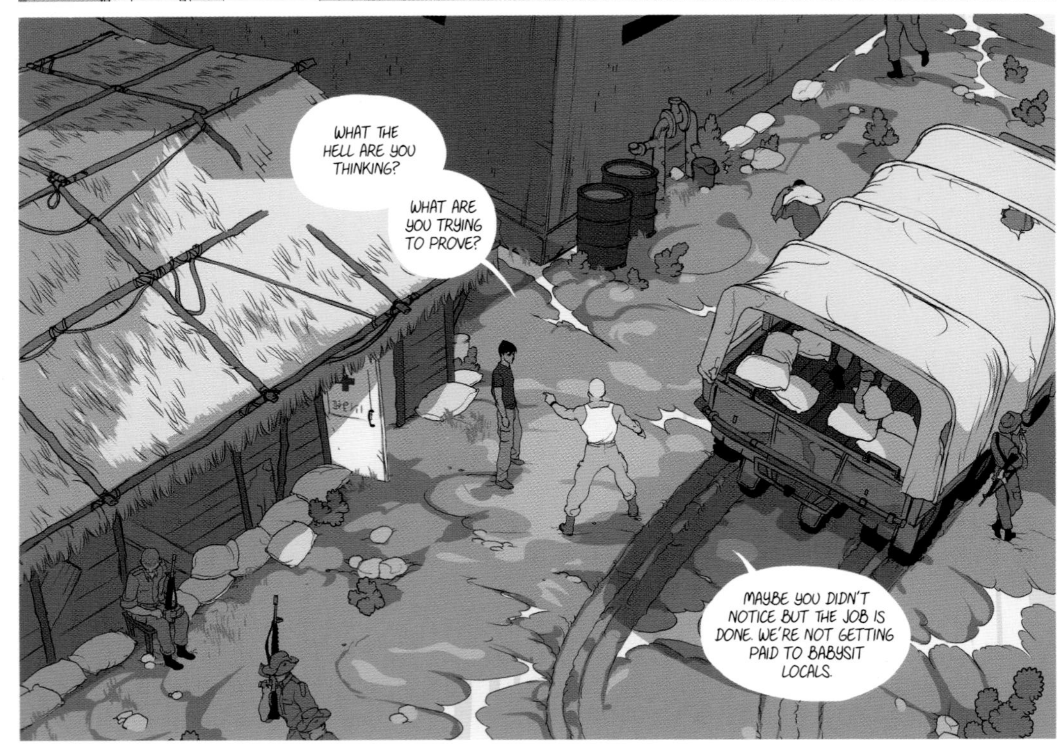
WHAT THE HELL ARE YOU THINKING?
WHAT ARE YOU TRYING TO PROVE?
MAYBE YOU DIDN'T NOTICE BUT THE JOB IS DONE. WE'RE NOT GETTING PAID TO BABYSIT LOCALS.

WE CAN'T JUST WALK AWAY...
YES, WE CAN.

THERE'S A WAR GOING ON HERE, IN CASE YOU DIDN'T NOTICE.

YOU SAID IT WAS A JOKE.

SO THEY PAID US EACH 22K MORE AS A JOKE? ARE YOU RETARDED?
THE WAR IS REAL. THIS KID IS PROBABLY A GUERRILLA OR A TERRORIST OR SOMETHING.

FINE. I'LL TAKE THIS "TERRORIST" BACK TO HIS PARENTS. BE BACK IN AN HOUR.
IT'S ONLY ABOUT THIRTY-FIVE MILES AWAY.

I'M WORRIED ABOUT YOU, MARK.

BBRUMM

SCREEECH!
WHAT THE HELL IS THAT?

DEMONS.

THERE'S NO WAY AROUND. WE'RE STUCK HERE.

MAN, THIS IS INSANE. NEVER SEEN ANYTHING LIKE THAT.

HOW THE HELL DID IT GET HERE? YOU'D NEED A TANK TO PULL THIS THING OUT OF THE GROUND.

WE DON'T LIKE INTERFERING WITH THESE POWERS....

IT'S FINE, WE'LL GO ON BY FOOT.

NO NO NO.
WE LEAVE THE BOY HERE. HE WILL FIND HIS WAY ALONE.

WHAT??

THEY ARE THREATENING US. THEY ARE TELLING US NOT TO GO ON.

WHO IS THREATENING US?

THE DIVINE.

WHAT THE HELL ARE YOU TALKING ABOUT?

SIRS, WE NEED TO LEAVE THIS PLACE.
LET'S GO BACK TO CAMP. EVERYTHING WILL BE FINE.
LET'S JUST LEAVE THE BOY HERE. HIS FRIENDS WILL TAKE CARE OF HIM. RIGHT, BOY?

HE'LL BE FINE, MARK. WE HAVE NOTHING TO GAIN FROM THIS.

CAN YOU WALK BY YOURSELF?
YES. THANK YOU, SIR, FOR HELPING.

THUMP!

C'MON, MAN!

GET IN THE JEEP! HE'LL BE FINE.

THE KID CAN'T WALK. I'M GOING WITH HIM.

WE CAN'T WAIT FOR YOU.
I DON'T WANT YOU TO WAIT.

THERE'S NO VILLAGE, NO PARENTS. THERE'S NOTHING, SIR, JUST KIDS.
THIS MAP IS.... IS NOT GOOD. AND THEY HAVE A DRAGON THAT PROTECTS THEM.

YOU SAID DRAGON?
IT'S A DEVILISH CREATURE, SOME SAY IT'S A SNAKE OUT OF THE CHINESE OCEAN, I REALLY DON'T KNOW, SIR.

YOU'RE MAKING A BIG MISTAKE, MAN.

GIVE ME THE PHONE.
YOU'RE NOT SUPPOSED TO USE IT.
DO YOU WANT ME TO BEG?

HELLO?

HEY HON.

MARK! ARE YOU OKAY? HOW IS VIETNAM?

I'M NOT IN VIETNAM, I'M IN... QUANLOM. I COULDN'T TELL YOU ABOUT IT WHEN I LEFT, BUT...

WHAT... ARE YOU TALKING ABOUT?

EVERYTHING IS OKAY. LISTEN, I'M HERE, IT'S ACTUALLY A U.S. GOVERNMENT OPERATION. LISTEN, THERE'S A KID HERE...
HE GOT HURT IN A MINEFIELD AND I...IT'S NO BIG DEAL, I'M TAKING HIM TO HIS PARENTS...

MINEFIELD? ARE YOU OKAY? WHAT'S GOING ON?

I'M OKAY. I JUST WANTED TO TELL YOU. I'LL BE CAREFUL, I PROMISE.

YOU CRAZY FUCKHEAD.
I'LL BE BACK AT THE CAMP IN A FEW HOURS.

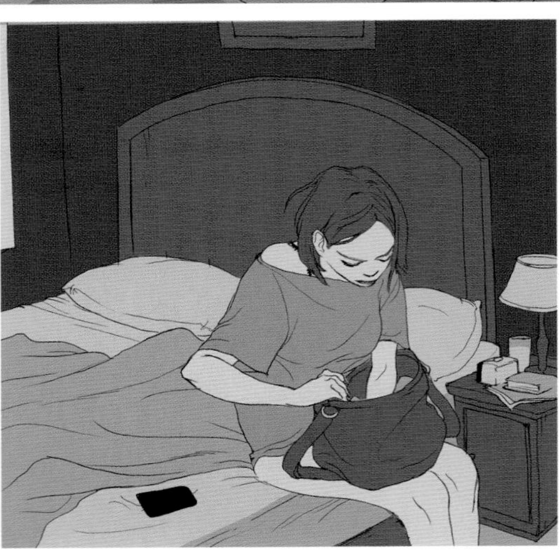

KCTX
ALLEN MCGONIGAL
TRAVEL AND TOURISM REPRTER
allenMcG@kctx.tv
785-558-6963

FOR BREAKING NEWS,
CALL US TOLL FREE
1-TV-TIPS-K

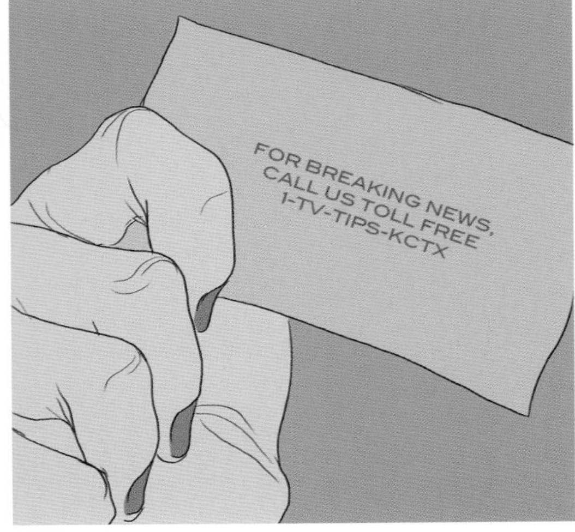
FOR BREAKING NEWS,
CALL US TOLL FREE
1-TV-TIPS-KCTX

PUNCH!!
KRK!
THICK
THUMP!
KRINKF!

HEY MARK!
CONGRATS, YOU'RE A FATHER NOW!
I...
HUH?
DON'T YOU RECOGNIZE ME?
HEY, CAN YOU CLOSE THE CURTAINS?
CAN YOU DO IT?
DRIP
WHA...

DRIP...
DR

DRIP... DROP.
IT'S TIME TO WAKE UP!
WHA—

WE SAW YOU PUT A BOMB IN OUR MOUNTAIN.
NOW YOU TELL US HOW TO TAKE IT APART. CAN YOU DO IT?

...WHAT...? YOU GOT THE WRONG GUY...

I JUST WANTED TO HELP A KID... WHERE IS HE?

HE IS BACK WITH HIS FAMILY.
NOW TELL US ABOUT THE BOMB.

I DON'T KNOW ANYTHING...

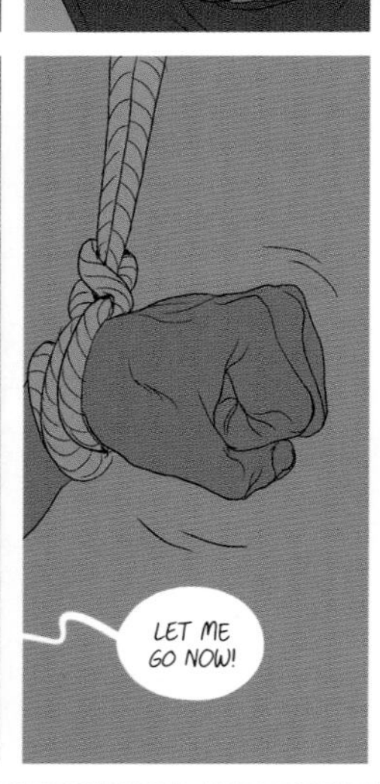
LET ME GO NOW!

COME ON... I KNOW YOU'RE A GOOD KID...
WHY ARE YOU—

CRACK!

FLAKK!

WE ARE NOT KIDS!

I'M 9 AND 7 MONTHS.

AND HE IS MY TWIN BROTHER, ONE MINUTE YOUNGER THAN ME.

BUT HE IS SMARTER.

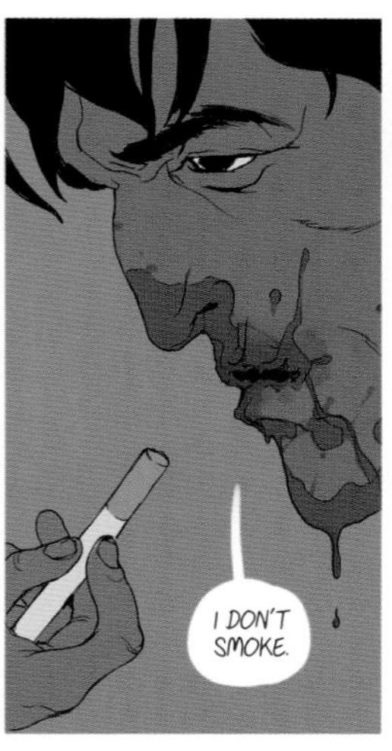
I DON'T SMOKE.

ONE MORE FOR ME!

MY NAME IS LUKE AND THIS IS THOMAS.

HE DOESN'T TALK BUT HE HAS MAGIC POWERS.

...RIGHT.

HE CAN TEAR THINGS APART. PULL THINGS OUT OF OTHER THINGS.
YOU MEAN LIKE UPROOTING A TREE IN THE MIDDLE OF THE ROAD?

YEAH!!
DID YOU SEE THAT?

LET'S CUT THE CRAP...
WHEN ARE YOU GOING TO LET ME GO?

DRAW US A MAP AND TELL US HOW TO DISARM THE BOMB.
THEN WE LET YOU GO.

I ALREADY TOLD YOU...
YOU'VE GOT THE WRONG GUY!

SO WHY DID YOU COME HERE?

I NEEDED THE MONEY... I JUST HELP WITH THE LOGISTICS.
BUT YOU ARE AMERICAN! YOU HAVE MONEY...
WELL... I DON'T.

I DON'T BELIEVE YOU.

YOU REALIZE THAT VERY SOON THE ARMY WILL COME LOOKING FOR ME, AND YOU WILL—

AARRRG!

WHAT THE FUCK?!

MY FINGER!!

IT'S MAGIC.

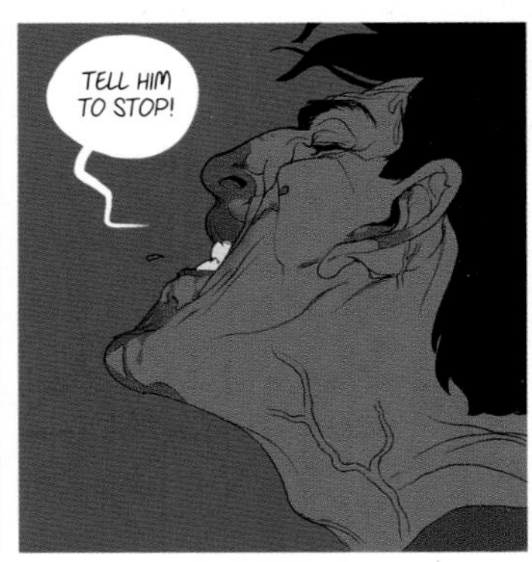
TELL HIM TO STOP!

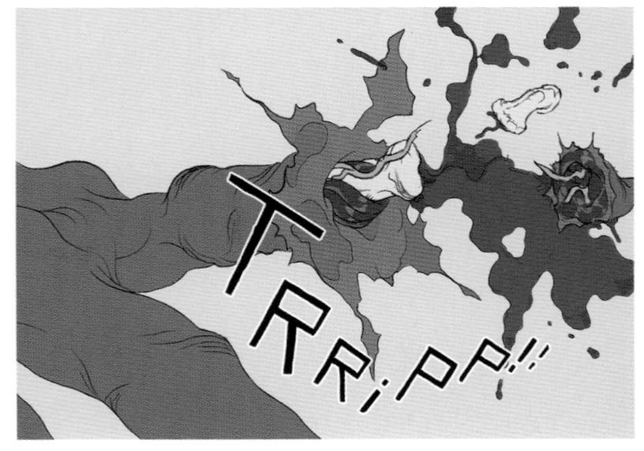
TRRIPP!!!

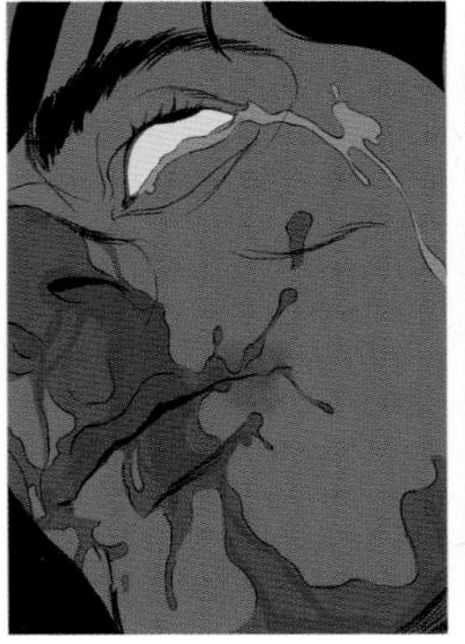

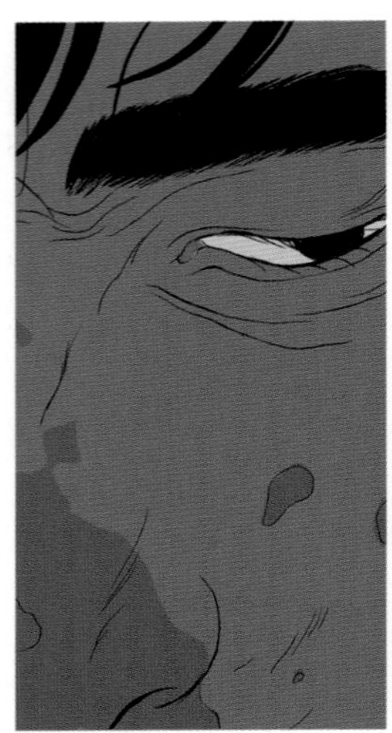
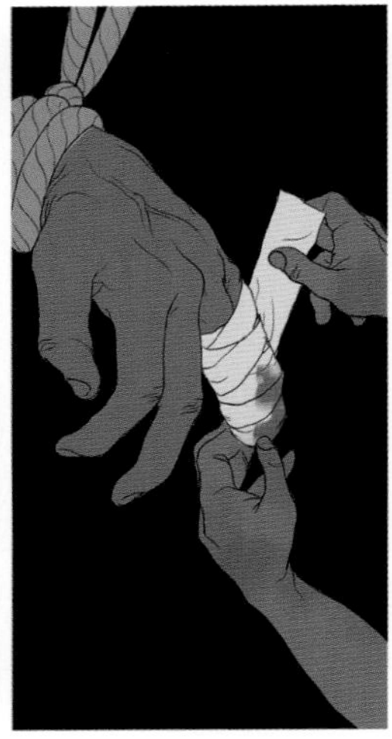

YOU...!
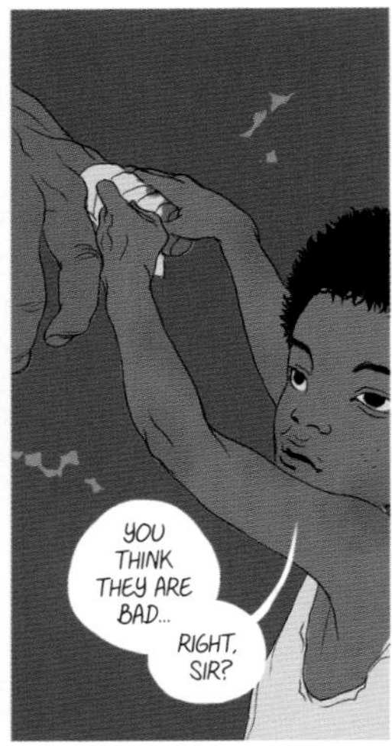
YOU THINK THEY ARE BAD...
RIGHT, SIR?

DID THEY HURT YOU?
THEY ARE GOOD, VERY GOOD.

AND THEY ARE MY FAMILY...
EVERYONE CALLS THEM "THE DIVINE."

THEY TOOK ME WITH THEM, AND GAVE ME FOOD AND SHELTER...

"THE DIVINE"?! THEY'RE A COUPLE OF CRAZY KIDS DRUNK WITH POWER.
THEY ARE BROTHERS TO DRAGONS AND COMPANIONS TO OWLS.
DRAGONS... AGAIN.

LOOK, SIR. OUR MOUNTAIN IS GUARDED BY LEH. ITS SPIRIT LIVES INSIDE.

IF THEY MAKE THE BOMB EXPLODE...
LEH'S SPIRIT WILL NOT HAVE A PLACE TO LIVE.

SO YOU WANT ME TO SAVE A DRAGON?
YOU SAVED ME... SO...

WHAT IF THERE'S NO DRAGON?

THERE IS. BUT WE'RE NOT ALLOWED TO SEE IT.

THEN HOW DO YOU KNOW HE'S REAL?

IF WE SEE HIM WE DIE.
EVEN SEEING A PICTURE OF HIM WOULD KILL US.

ONE TIME, ONE OF THE KIDS DREW LEH ON A TREE.
YOU KNOW WHAT HAPPENED?

HE BECAME BLIND. THEN HE DIED.

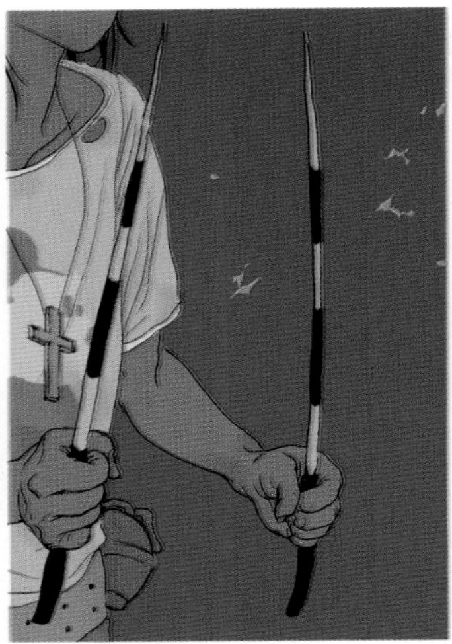

I'M ON YOUR SIDE.

BECAUSE YOU THINK WE ARE KIDS.
YOU LIKE KIDS, YOU ARE NOT AFRAID OF KIDS.
WELL, ACTUALLY...

YOU CAN HELP US WIN, OR YOU CAN STAY HERE.
BUT IF YOU STAY HERE, WE TAKE OUT YOUR EYES. BECAUSE YOU SAW US.

STOP!!!

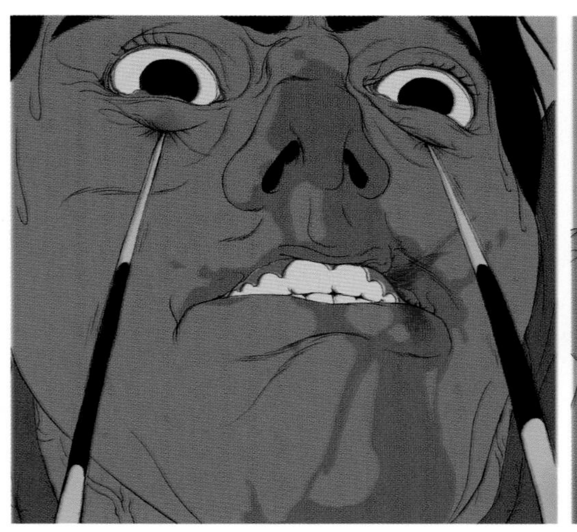

WE ARE AN ARMY. WE FIGHT FOR QUANLOM FREEDOM.
WE DON'T CARE ABOUT OLD PEOPLE BEGGING.

I WAS A SOLDIER TOO, YOU KNOW
REALLY? DID YOU KILL PEOPLE?

NO, I WAS JUST... A TECHNICIAN. WAIT...
WHAT?
I'LL HELP YOU.

I SAID I'LL DO IT.

SOMEONE SHOULD HELP YOU. I GUESS IT'S GONNA BE ME.

GIVE US YOUR WORD! AS AN AMERICAN SOLDIER...

YOU HAVE IT.

CUTT

BUT THERE IS ONE CONDITION: NO MAPS...
I'M GOING TO DO IT MYSELF.

HOW CAN WE TRUST YOU?

YOU ALREADY TRUST ME. YOU JUST UNTIED ME.

WE CAN PUT YOU BACK ON THAT TREE.

HERE'S HOW WE'RE GONIG TO DO IT—

WE GO BACK TO THE TUBE TOGETHER, I DISARM THE BOMB.

THEN YOU GO BACK TO THE JUNGLE.

AND I GO BACK HOME.

DEAL?

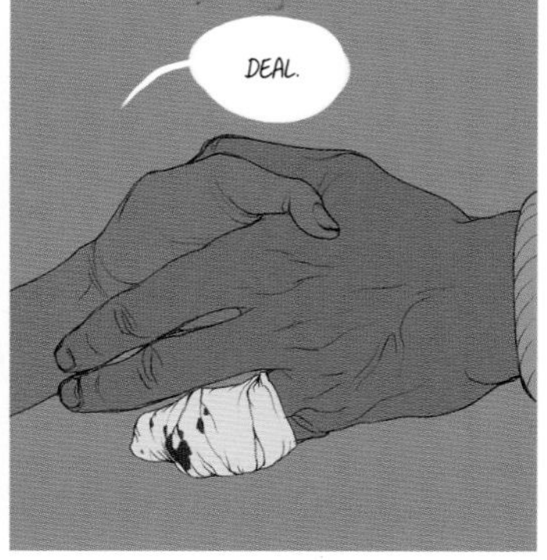
DEAL.

CAN YOU WALK?

YES, I COULD WALK BEFORE TOO, BUT I WANTED YOU TO COME HERE.
WHY?

BECAUSE YOU ARE GOOD, LIKE US. THE OTHER AMERICAN IS BAD...

JUST DOING OUR JOB, THAT'S ALL...

STOP!
IT'S A MINEFIELD.

WE SHOULD GO AROUND. IT'S TOO DANGEROUS.

IT WILL TAKE HOURS. WE DON'T HAVE TIME.

THOMAS WILL KEEP US SAFE.

YOUR BROTHER IS GOING TO GET KILLED!

SHHH! HE NEEDS TO CONCENTRATE NOW!

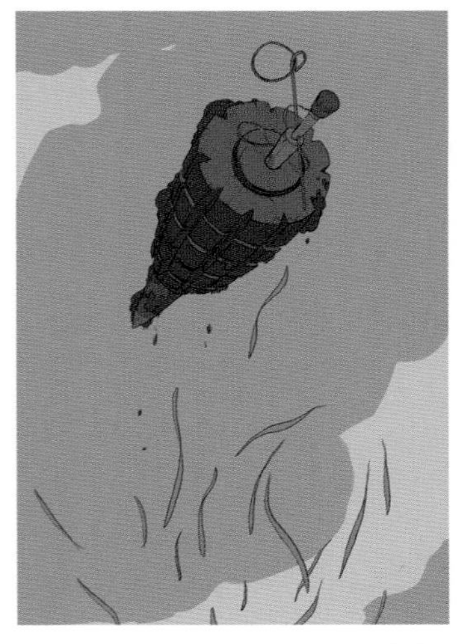

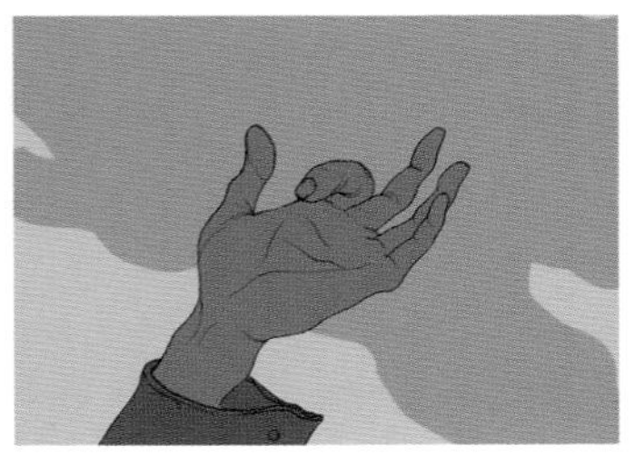

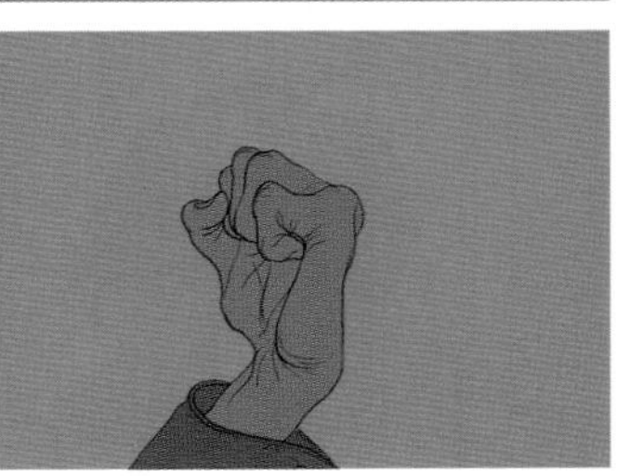

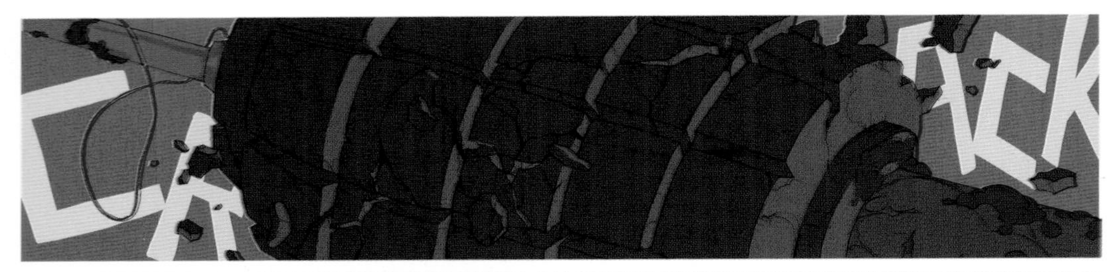

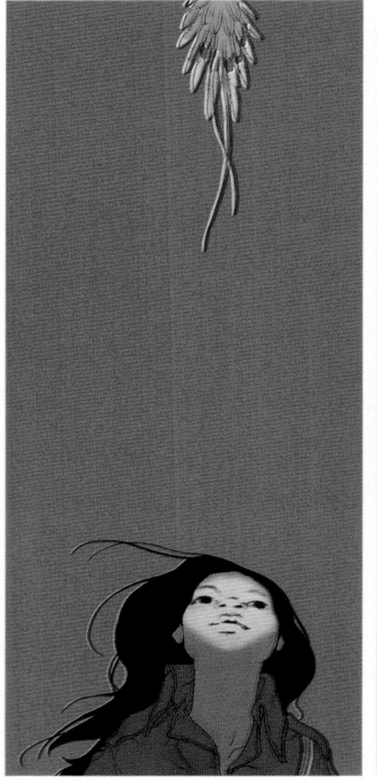

TOLD YOU! BROTHERS TO DRAGONS AND COMPANIONS TO OWLS.

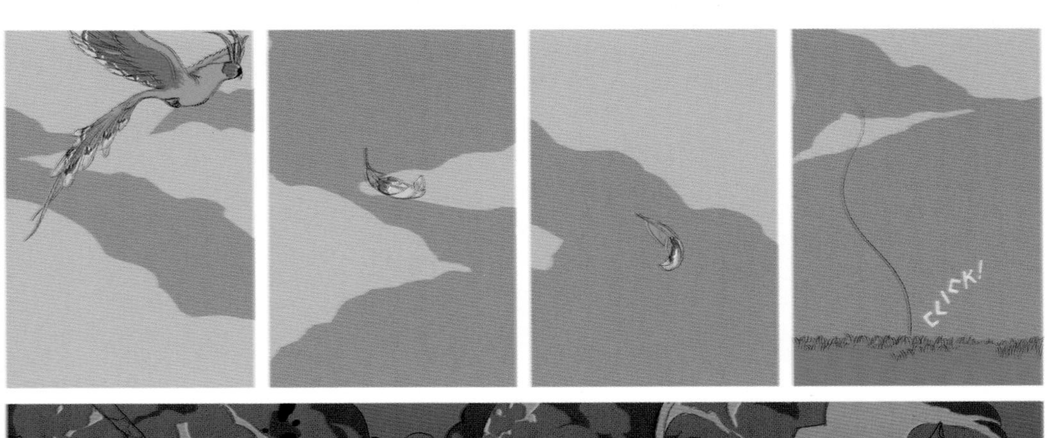
CLICK!

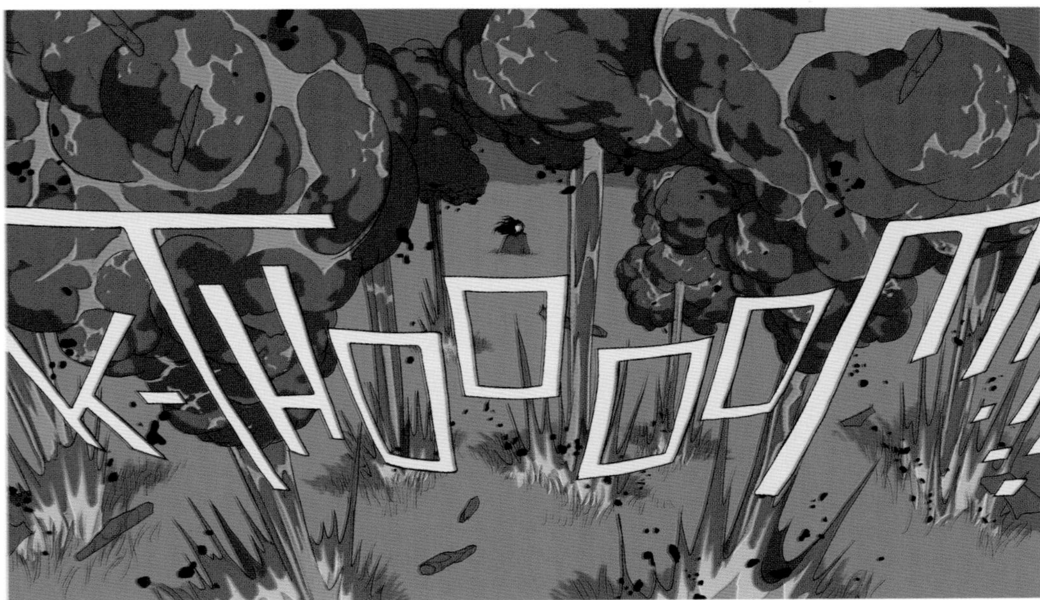
K-THOOOOOM!

CAN WE GO NOW?

THIS IS IT!

FINALLY.

WE COULDN'T VISIT FOR MONTHS...
BECAUSE OF THE MINES?

NO.
THE DIVINE SAID WE CAN GO BACK ONLY WHEN LEH CALLS...

YOU USED TO LIVE HERE?
YES. UNTIL THE ARMY CAME ONE MORNING AND TOLD EVERYONE TO LEAVE...

THEY WANTED TO MINE THE MOUNTAIN BUT THE VILLAGE WAS IN THE WAY.

SOME OF THE PEOPLE REFUSED SO THEY PUT THEM IN BIG TRUCKS... WE NEVER SAW THEM AGAIN.

...THEY TOOK MY PARENTS.

LATER WE FOUND OUT THEY WERE KILLED IN QUANLOM CITY.
...I'M SORRY.

THE DIVINE'S FAMILY, TOO... BUT THEIR FATHER—

HE FOUGHT BACK, TRIED TO RESIST.

SO THE SOLDIERS PUSHED HIM OFF THE MOUNTAINTOP... DOWN TO THE ROCKS.

HE SURVIVED THE FALL BUT STARVED TO DEATH IN A WEEK.

WE COULD SEE HIM FROM ABOVE, BUT COULDN'T DO ANYTHING TO HELP HIM.

SO WE HID IN THE WOODS. THEY SAID TIME WILL COME AND WE WILL TAKE BACK LEH'S HOME, AND OUR VILLAGE WILL BE BUILT AGAIN.

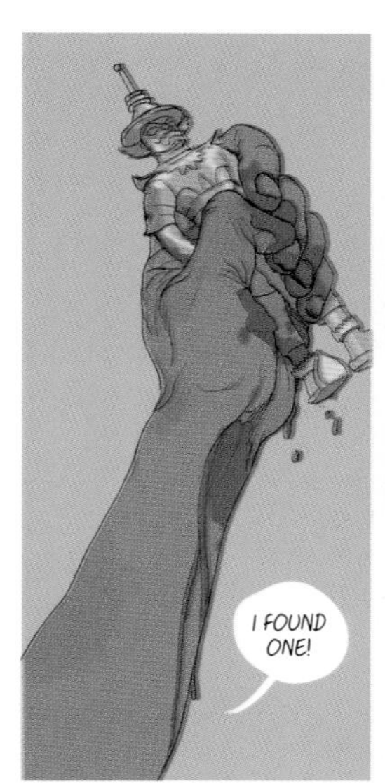
I FOUND ONE!

HERE'S ANOTHER ONE!
THREE!!

LEH'S WARRIORS. THEY'VE BEEN WAITING FOR US HERE.

WE'RE READY. LET'S GO STOP THE BOMB!

WAIT FOR ME.
WE'LL BE WATCHING YOU. DON'T FORGET YOUR PROMISE.

WHAT IS THIS??

TOCOTOCOTOC
TOCOTOCOTOKTAC
THE ARMY IS HERE...
YOU BETRAYED US! BROKE YOUR WORD!
I DIDN'T! LISTEN, YOU HAVE TO GET EVERYBODY OFF THE TOP OF THE MOUNTAIN NOW!
THEY'RE GOING TO BLOW IT UP!

TOCOTOCKTOCO
BUT YOU SAID YOU WOULD STOP IT!

WE'RE TOO LATE... THEY CAN DETONATE THE BOMB FROM THE HELICOPTER.

THOMAS WILL TAKE IT APART.

DO IT! YOU HAVE TO GO FAST, THOMAS. NOW!!

WAIT... STOP! IT'S MY FRIEND!
JASON!

DON'T DO IT!!

TOCO TOCO TOCO
TOCOTOCOT
HOOM

SON OF A BITCH...

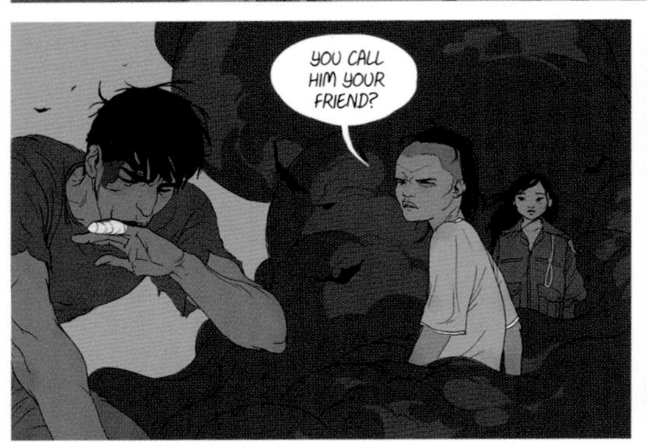
YOU CALL HIM YOUR FRIEND?

WHERE'S THE BOY?

NO... NO...

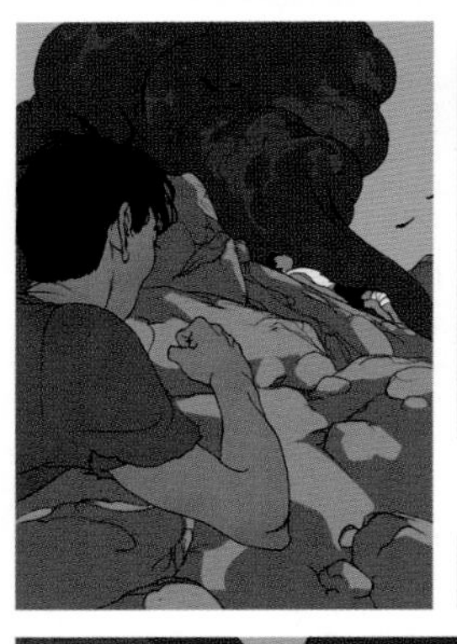

HEY!

HE'S DEAD.

THE MAN WHO DID THIS... WE MUST FIND HIM, AND FEED HIM TO LEH.
GOD, CUT THIS CRAP. I DON'T WANT TO HEAR ABOUT YOUR DRAGON.

YOUR FRIEND RUINED LEH'S HOME AND NOW HIS SPIRIT HAS NO PLACE... HE WILL NOT REST... UNTIL HE FEEDS.
THEN EVERYTHING WILL BE GOOD AGAIN.

YOU WANT TO SACRIFICE JASON TO YOUR DRAGON GOD?
IS THAT WHAT YOU'RE SAYING?

YES.
WE'RE GOING TO YOUR FRIEND'S CAMP RIGHT NOW.
YOU'RE INSANE! THERE'S A WHOLE ARMY OVER THERE.

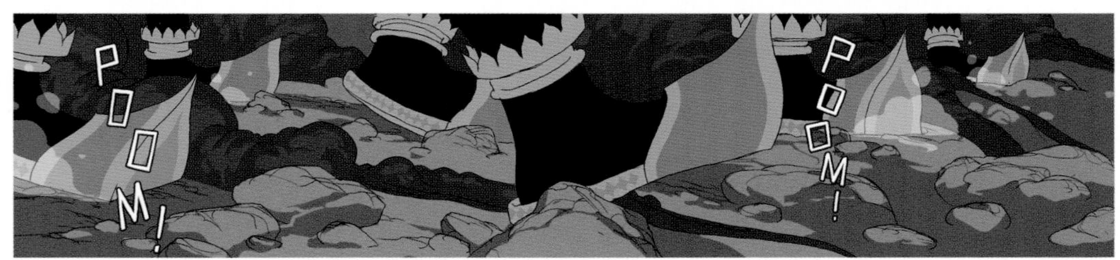
POOM!
POOM!

WE HAVE OUR ARMY TOO... WILL YOU COME WITH US?

COME.
POOM!
POOM!

POOM!
POOM!
POOM!

I LOVE QUANLOM NIGHTS.

YOU KNOW WHAT WE SAY ABOUT THE NIGHTS HERE?
TELL ME.

"NIGHT IS A BLESSING, UNTIL YOU COME ACROSS SOMEONE WITH BETTER EYESIGHT."
THAT'S A GOOD ONE. LUCKY FOR ME I HAVE TWENTY-TWENTY VISION.
BUT WHAT ABOUT YOUR FRIEND?

HE MADE HIS CHOICE.

SO YOU'RE LEAVING HIM BEHIND?

NOT LEAVING ANYONE. WE HAVE A FLIGHT TO CATCH TOMORROW FROM QUANLOM CITY.

HEY, WHAT'S THAT OVER THERE?

POOOM!

POOOM!

IT'S THEM!
THEM?

FFTT
POOM!
POOM!
POOM!

CRACKSH!

KKRASH!

EEEE!! EEE!! EEE

SPING
FINGG!

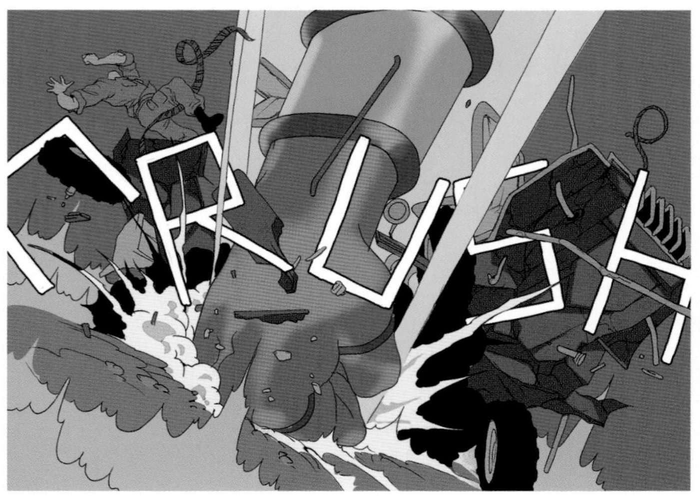
CRUSH

AIM FOR THE HEAD. YOU GOT ONE CHANCE. DON'T BLOW IT!

NOW!

TSHHHOOOMFFF

KA-BLAST!!!

I KNEW IT! WE'RE TAKING THEM DOWN...

AIM FOR
THE HEADS!!

IS THIS
THE MAN WHO
BOMBED US?

I DON'T THINK HE'S IN CHARGE HERE ANYMORE...
IT'S HIM!

DON'T YOU THINK YOUR BROTHER IS A BIT OUT OF CONTROL?
HE IS DOING WHAT NEEDS TO BE DONE.

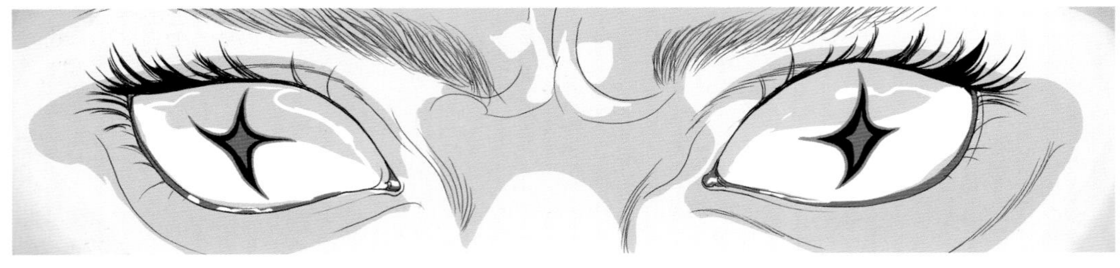

BBOUM

CRACK!
BREAK!

THAT LITTLE WITCH IS RIGHT IN FRONT OF US.
KILL HIM!

KRRIPPP

RAPPPK
KRACK
CRI

DAMN!

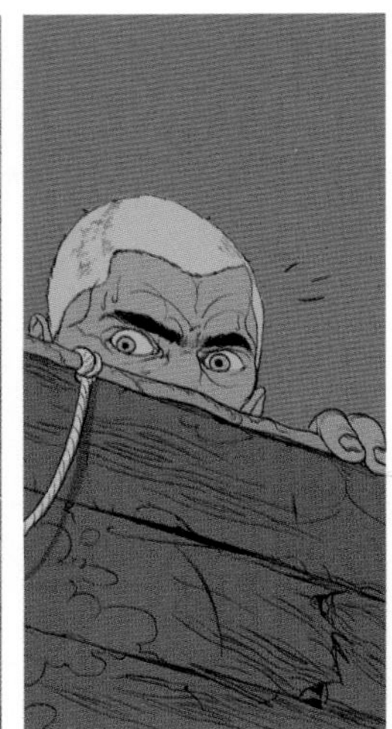

WE NEED
HIM ALIVE!

TELL HIM TO STOP. YOU GOT EVERYTHING YOU WANTED, YOU DESTROYED THIS PLACE, YOU HAD YOUR REVENGE!

IT'S ALL RIGHT, IT'S ALL RIGHT.
EVERYTHING IS OKAY.
YOU'RE NOT ALONE, IT'S ALL RIGHT!

CHOOM
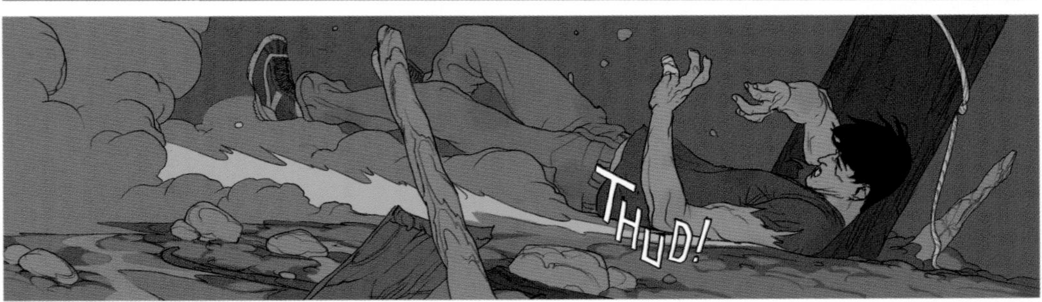
THUD!

VVVOOOOM!
FOOOMM

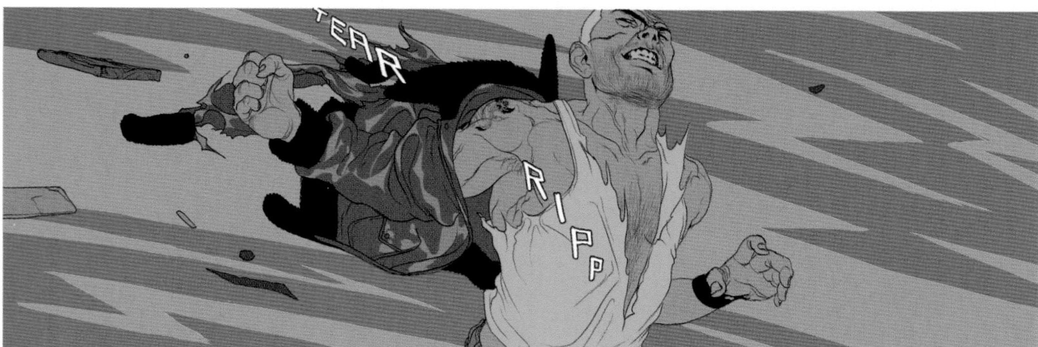
TEAR
RIPP

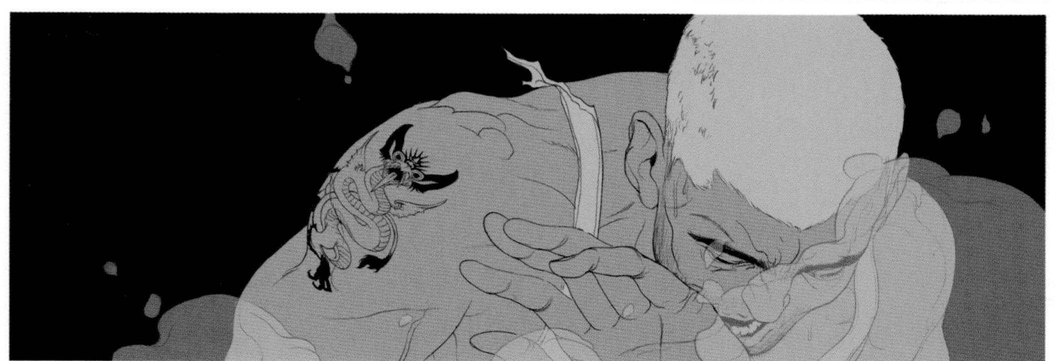

TUMBLE!

YOUR FRIEND... HE IS PROTECTED BY LEH...
YOU CAN'T BE SERIOUS.

THERE... ON HIS SHOULDER.
RIIPP

I'M NOT SURE WHAT...

I'M PROTECTED BY IT!
IT'S JUST A FUCKING TATTOO!

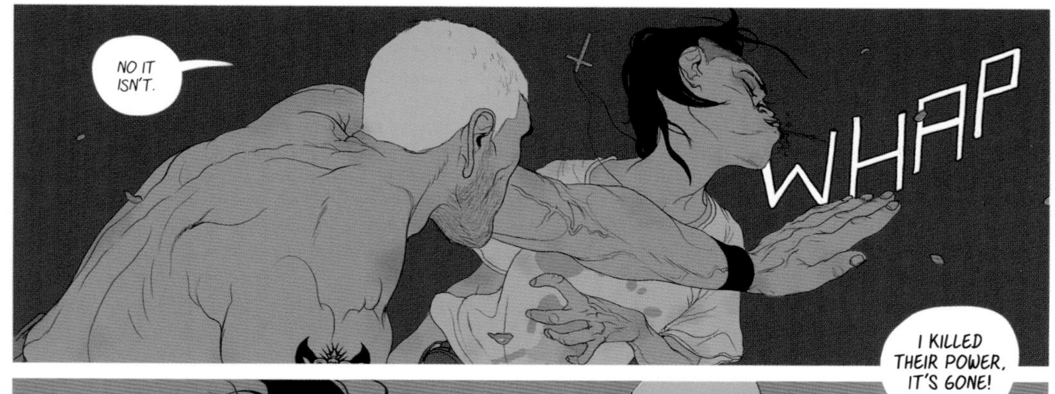
NO IT ISN'T.
WHAP

I KILLED THEIR POWER, IT'S GONE!
SLAP

STOP!!

RELAX, BRO.
YOU'RE JUST IN TIME. THAT'S OUR RIDE BACK TO THE CITY.
IT LEAVES IN 30 MINUTES. WE'LL TAKE THEM WITH US.

WHAT FOR? JUST LET THEM GO. THEY WON'T TOUCH YOU NOW.
NO... THEY SHOULD BE PUNISHED.

CLINK
THEY WILL BE HANGED...
ONE BY ONE.
CHLAK

TRUST ME.

NOW THAT'S A BEAUTY!

MAN, THIS IS GOING TO BE PERFECT ON MY BEDSIDE TABLE. CHICKS LOVE THIS STUFF.

TOCTOCTOCTOco TOC TOC

DID YOU KNOW HE HAD IT?
HAD WHAT?

THE SIGN... LEH.
YEAH... HE SHOWED THAT TO ME.

WHY DIDN'T YOU TELL US?
I DIDN'T THINK IT MATTERED.

YOU WERE WRONG.
HE GOT LEH DRAWN ON HIS ARM AND WE ALL SAW IT AND WE'RE GONNA DIE NOW.

YOU THINK IT'S A GAME?
THIS IS THE REAL WORLD.
THERE ARE NO DRAGONS AND NO "FRIENDS OF DRAGONS"...
TOCTOCTOCTOCTOC TOCTOC
THAT "SIGN" IS JUST A STUPID DRAWING.

AND YOU'RE JUST KIDS LOST IN A JUNGLE.

THIS IS NO GAME... WHAT THOMAS DID WAS REAL! YOU SAW IT!

MAYBE I WAS LOST, TOO.

CRACK!

WHAT THE HELL WAS THAT?
SOMETHING HIT US!
WHAT??
SOMETHING BIG...
I DON'T SEE ANYTHING... JUST DON'T LOSE CONTROL!

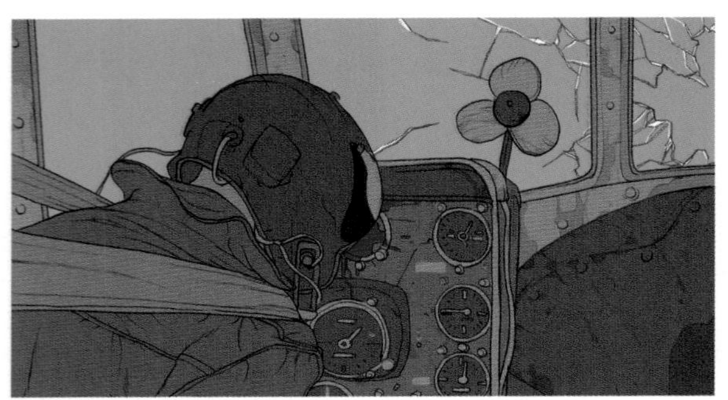

WHAT THE HELL IS THIS?

WAIT, I GET IT.

LIZARD WANTS TO SETTLE THE SCORE!

C'MON, SHOW YOUR UGLY FACE...

OH... SHIT.

IT'S LEH!

KONGG
KRRAFF!

TTOCTAKKOCTTKKK

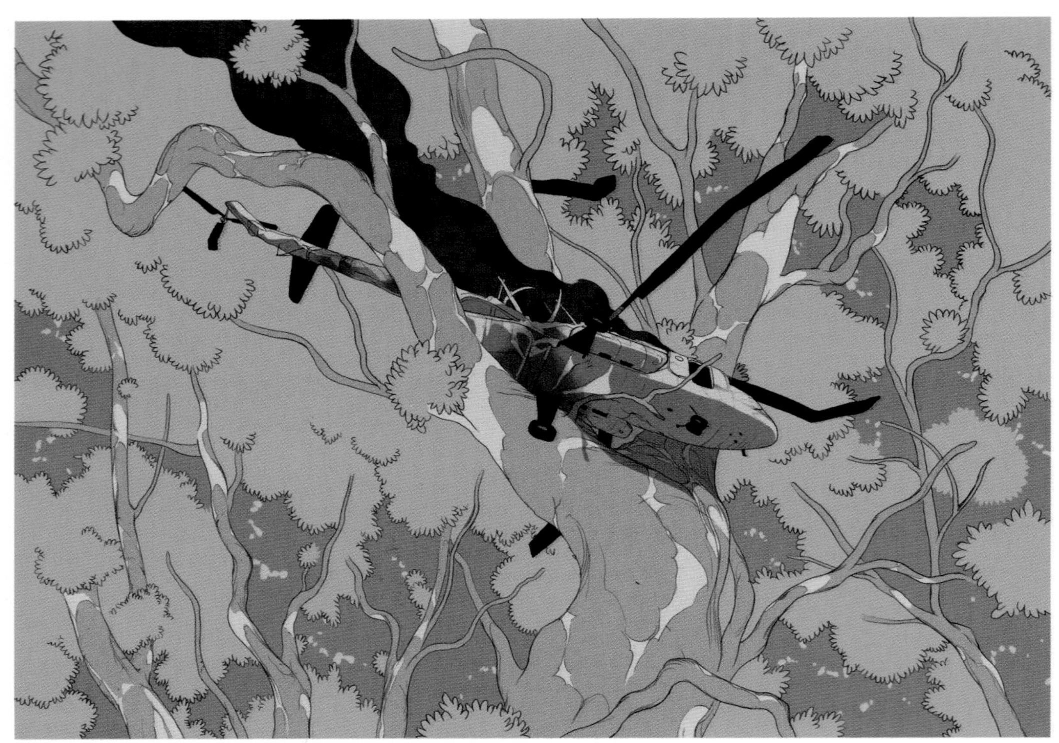

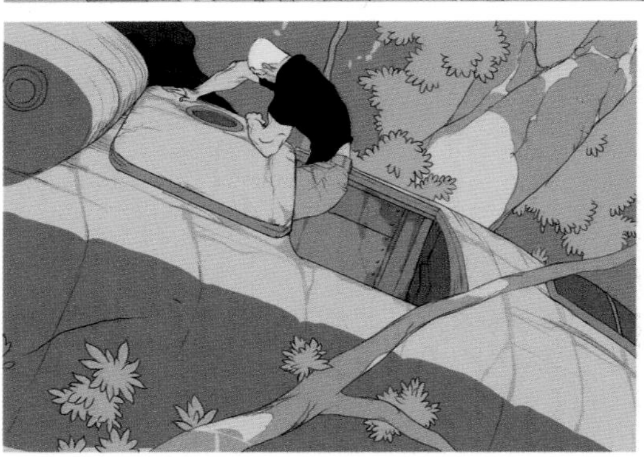

YOU COMING?
WHAT ABOUT THE KIDS? YOU GOTTA LET THEM GO!

I DON'T GIVE A FUCK ABOUT THEM.

JUST THROW ME THE KEYS!

FUCK THE KEYS. SEE YOU LATER.

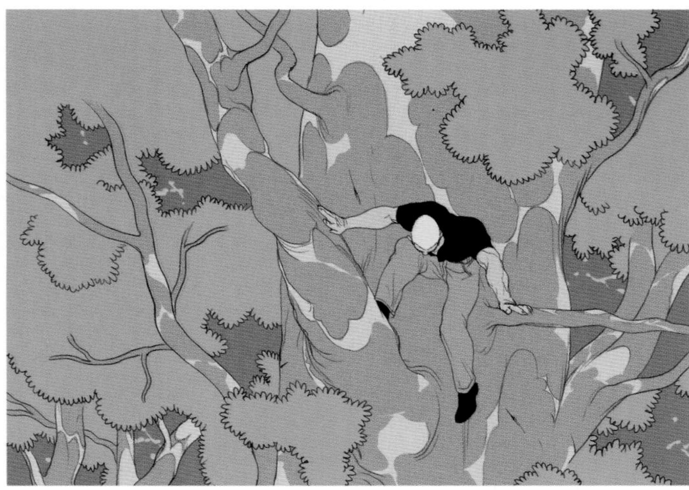

KCHAN!
THANG!

CAN'T YOU DO YOUR THING AND GET THIS THING OFF?

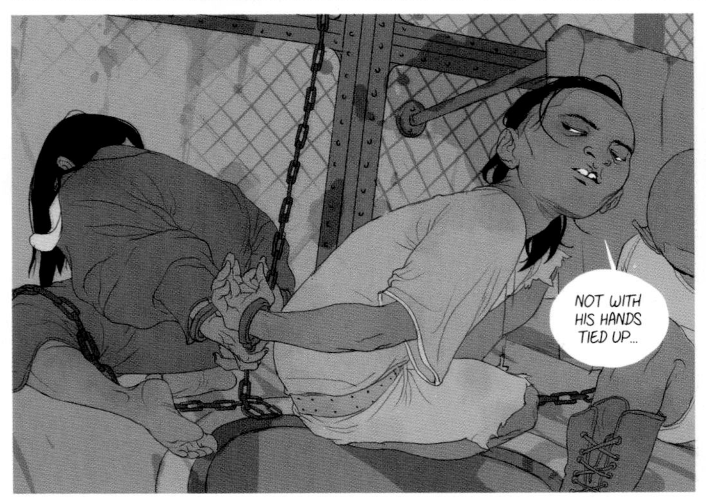
NOT WITH HIS HANDS TIED UP...

GODDAMMIT.

YOU FUCKING PIECE OF SHIT.

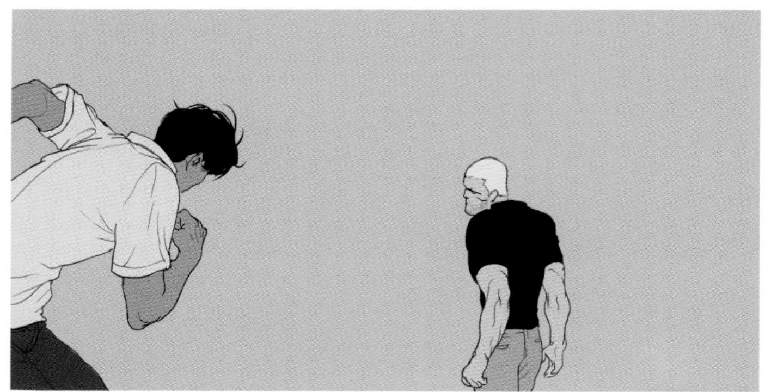

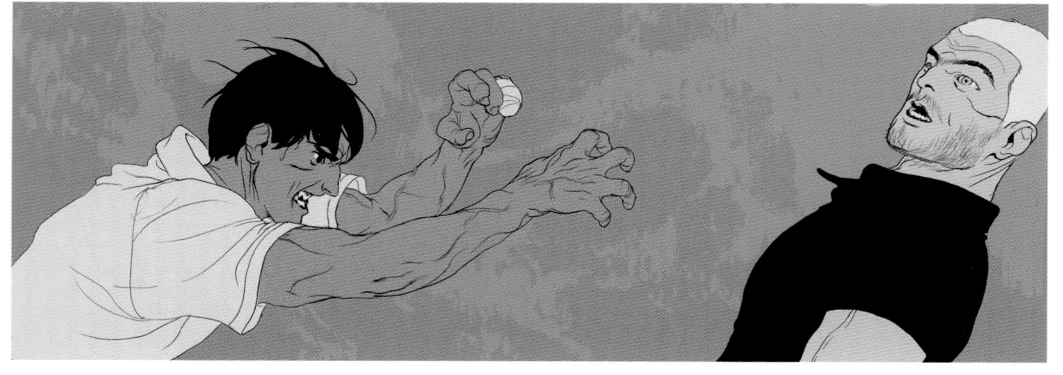

WHERE ARE THE KEYS?

SO YOU CHOOSE THESE KIDS OVER ME?
THAK

I WAS WRONG ABOUT YOU.

NOW CHILL OUT, OR I'M GOING FOR YOUR SHIUTU POINT. GOT IT?
CLICK!

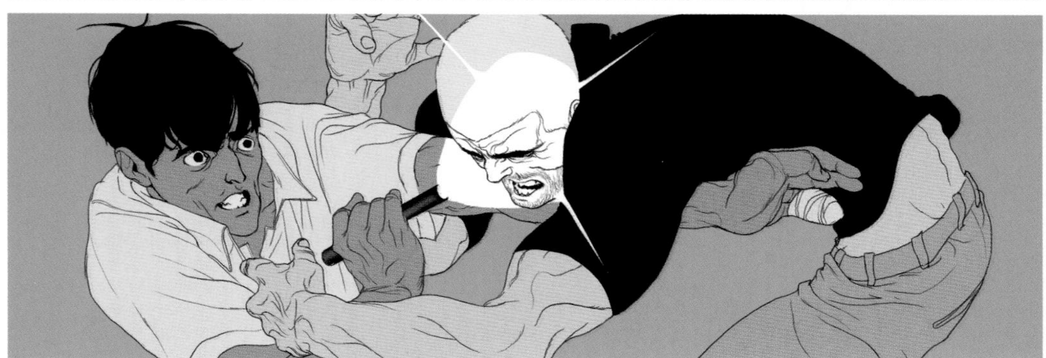

PPTCH!

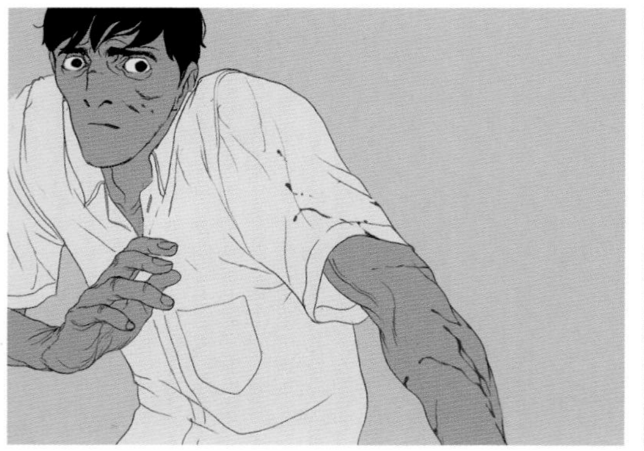

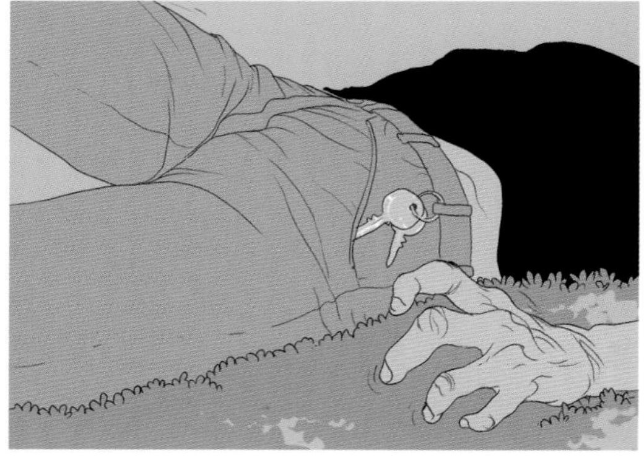

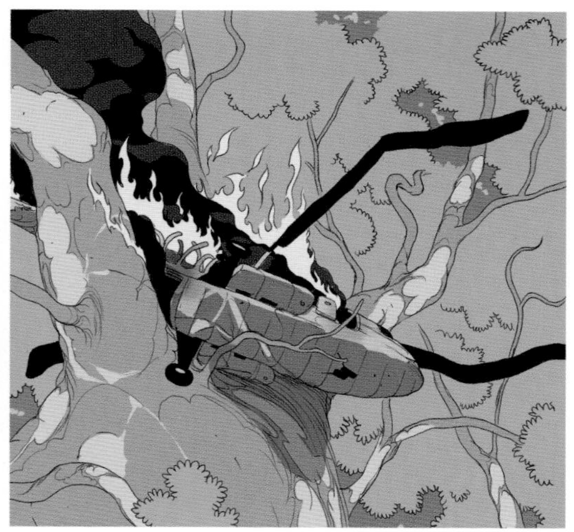

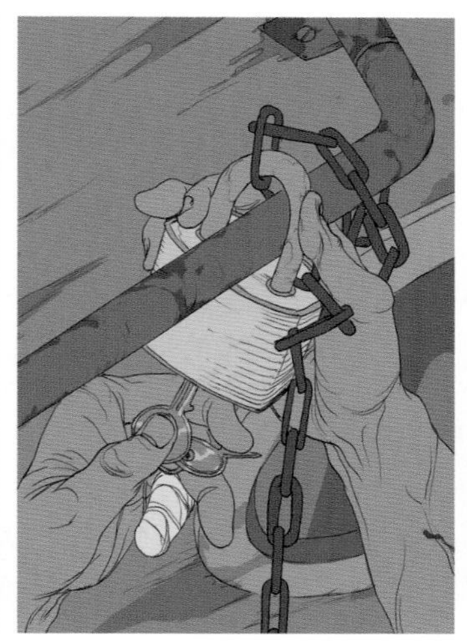

IS HE DEAD?

ALMOST, I THINK. HE'S STILL BREATHING.
GOOD. HE'LL BE HERE SOON.
WHO WILL?

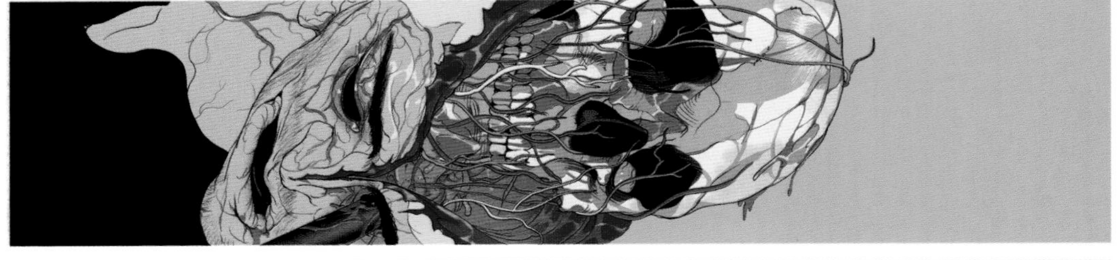

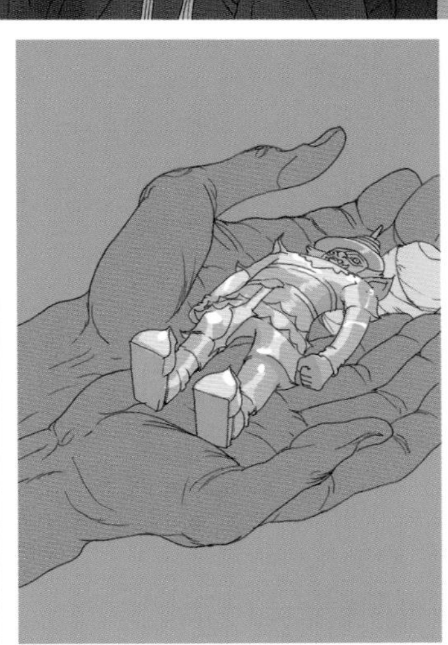

A GIFT,
FOR YOUR CHILD.

DEPARTURE
FOLLOWING EXTREME POLITICAL PRESSURE, THE PRESIDENT OF THE UNITED STATES HAS DECLARED THAT ALL OPERATIONS IN QUANLOM WILL BE STOPPED INDEFINITELY.

THE ENTIRE DEMOLISHED AREA IS TO BE RESTORED, VILLAGES ARE TO BE REBUILT, AND LOCAL CHILDREN ARE TO BE GIVEN IMMEDIATE SHELTER.

AND IT'S THE WIFE OF ONE OF THE AMERICAN AGENTS IN QUANLOM WHO FOREVER CHANGED THE FATE OF THESE CHILDREN BY MAKING A SINGLE PHONE CALL TO A LOCAL TEXAS TV STATION, TURNING THIS HIGHLY SENSITIVE INFORMATION INTO A WORLDWIDE TRENDING TOPIC.

I HAVE NO IDEA WHERE HE IS RIGHT NOW. I DID THIS... ENTIRELY WITHOUT HIS KNOWLEDGE.

DEPARTURE
FLIGHT
TIME
DESTENATION
0 6 0:1:54 L
0 0 3 1:1:30 N
0 7 4 2:3:05 J

CNN
HE MUST HAVE KNOWN I WOULD RAISE HELL WHEN HE CALLED ME FROM OVER THERE. NO CHILD SHOULD BE A SOLDIER. AND WE CERTAINLY SHOULDN'T BE FIGHTING AGAINST CHILDREN.

CNN
BUT RIGHT NOW I JUST WANT HIM BACK HOME WITH ME. SO WE CAN GO ON WITH OUR LIVES.

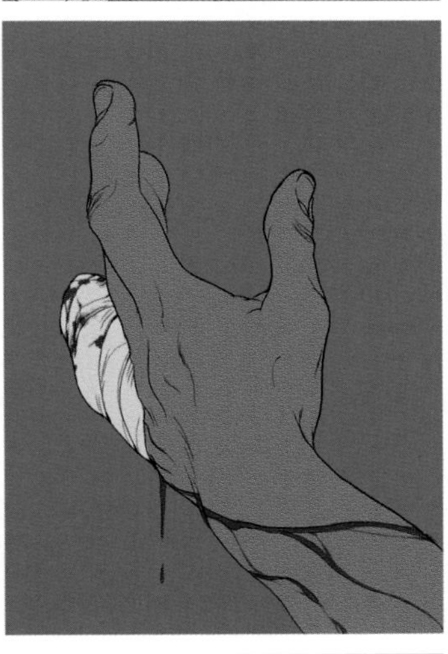

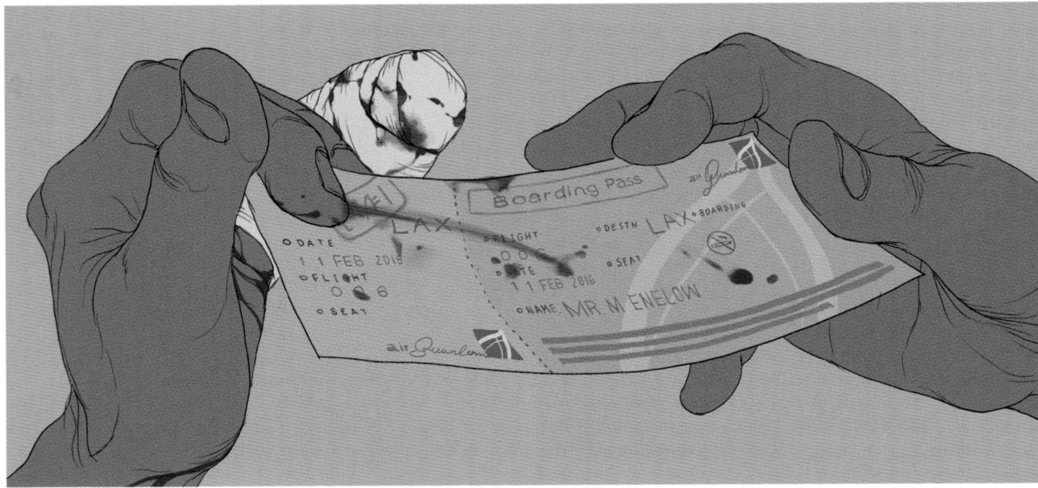
Boarding Pass
LAX
DATE
11 FEB 2016
FLIGHT
SEAT
DESTN
LAX
BOARDING
NAME
11 FEB 2016

YES, MR. NAKAMOTO, YOUR TICKETS ARE READY...

YES, IT IS INCLUDED IN THE VACATION PACKAGE.

LET ME KNOW IF THERE'S A PROBLEM WITH THAT, OKAY?
Mommy, look!
TRAVEL with RACHEL ENELOW.COM

OH, IT'S BEAUTIFUL, HONEY.
You know what it is?

I'M SO SORRY, SWEETHEART, BUT I'M REALLY BUSY RIGHT NOW.
WHY DON'T YOU GO SHOW DADDY! HE'S SITTING OUTSIDE.
Okay.

Daddy! Look at this!

You know what it is?
HMMM...

A MOUNTAIN. A VOLCANO.
...It's a—

...No, it's a—
OF COURSE IT'S A VOLCANO. DON'T YOU SEE?
But Daddy!

YOU KNOW I'VE BEEN TO A VOLCANO ONCE?
Really??

YEAH... IT WAS A LONG TIME AGO.
Were you alone?

NO, I HAD A FRIEND WITH ME.
Did you bring anything back for me? A volcano rock?

HAHA, NO, I WENT THERE BEFORE YOU WERE EVEN BORN.
BEFORE WE MOVED HERE TO EDEN...
YOU KNOW WHAT? I THINK I DID BRING YOU SOMETHING.

THIS IS FOR YOU.
Wow!

IT'S BEDTIME, YOU TWO! MARK, COULD YOU GIVE HIM A BATH WHILE I WRAP THIS UP?
SURE.

Can I take Daddy's present with me?
YEAH, WHY NOT.

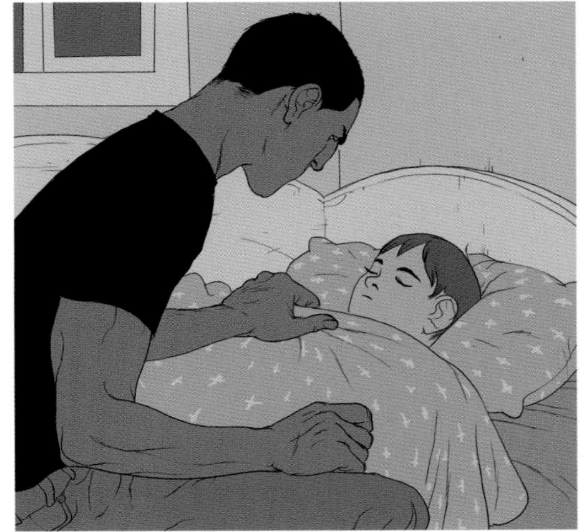

Daddy, I can't sleep.

JUST HOLD THIS TIGHT AND CLOSE YOUR EYES.

Did you really bring it from a volcano?
OF COURSE I DID.

Daddy?
YES?

I'm dreaming now.

THE END

© AP/SIPA

In January 2000, Associated Press photographer Apichart Weerawong took a photo of two twelve-year-old twins. It was taken immediately following the raid of a hospital by the Thai army, where those twins held 800 people as hostages. Weerawong's photo was quickly distributed all over the world, becoming an unparalleled image of childhood without childhood: chain-smoking child-soldiers, their eyes as tired as if they were fifty years older. Like many others, we were captivated by this photo. For several years we would take a look at it from time to time, trying to decipher it, learn something about childhood, about life in extreme circumstances, and about ourselves.

The twins in the photo are Johnny and Luther Htoo. During the late 1990s they led a group of hundreds of Karen refugees from east Burma, called "God's Army," and fought the Burmese army for dispossessing them from their lands. The Htoo twins were surrounded by legends: it was said they had magical powers, that they were invulnerable to bullets and mines, that they knew the Bible by heart without even reading it once. When we started working on this book, we drew our very first inspiration from these legends and from Weerawong's photo, but we took it to a place which is completely our own: it has become fiction. Luther now lives in Sweden, and Johnny lives in a Thai refugee camp, waiting to reunite with his mother in New Zealand. For us, however, they will always be twelve-year-olds, in a photo we'll never quite understand.

Asaf, Boaz, and Tomer, 2014

Executive Producer
RON PROPPER

Published by First Second
First Second is an imprint of Roaring Brook Press, a division of Holtzbrinck Publishing Holdings Limited Partnership
175 Fifth Avenue, New York, New York 10010

Cataloging-in-Publication Data is on file at the Library of Congress.

ISBN: 978-1-59643-674-9

First Second books may be purchased for business or promotional use. For information on bulk purchases please contact Macmillan Corporate and Premium Sales Department at (800) 221-7945 x5442 or by email at specialmarkets@macmillan.com.

First edition 2015
Cover Design and Logotype by Avi Neeman
Typeset in "HanukaEng" designed by Ben Nathan
Book design by Casey Gonzalez, John Green, and Danielle Ceccolini
Printed in China by Toppan Leefung Printing Ltd., Dongguan City, Guangdong Province

10 9 8 7 6 5 4 3 2 1